THE SMART Parent

Strategies for the Middle Years (8-12)

GARY & ANNE MARIE
EZZO

Multnomah Publishers *Sisters, Oregon*

THE SMART PARENT

published by Multnomah Books
a division of Multnomah Publishers, Inc.

© 1998 by Gary and Anne Marie Ezzo
International Standard Book Number: 1-57673-228-2

Cover photograph © 1998 by Greg Schneider

Unless otherwise noted, Scripture quotations are from:
The Holy Bible, New King James Version (NKJV) © 1984
by Thomas Nelson, Inc.

Printed in the United States of America

For information:
Multnomah Publishers, Inc.
Post Office Box 1720
Sisters, Oregon 97759

Library of Congress Cataloging–in–Publication Data
Ezzo, Gary.
    The smart parent: strategies for the middle years, ages
eight–twelve/by Gary and Anne Marie Ezzo.   p.cm.
    ISBN 1-57673-228-2   1. Preteens--United States.
    2. Parenting--United States.   3. Adolescent psychology--
    United States. 4. Communication in the family--United
    States. I. Ezzo, Anne Marie. II. Title
HQ777.15.E93   1998   98-10470
649'.124--dc21   CIP

98 99 00 01 02 03 04 – 10 9 8 7 6 5 4 3 2 1

The Smart Parent

TABLE OF CONTENTS

dedicated to Clifford and Wilma Olson
who faithfully guided us through
the middle years

INTRODUCTION

Consider these facts:

Tracking done by the Helen Dwight Reed Educational Foundation reveals that today there are nearly one million therapists at some level of professional standing, attempting to counsel over sixteen million Americans. Fixing this country's emotional problems after they have developed costs over 11 billion dollars a year according to the *Los Angles Times* (May 19, 1996).

According to a report in *Men's Health* (June 1995), heart disease affects one out of six American adult males, yet risk of heart attack could be reduced by 70 percent if men would practice basic preventative measures. Similarly, The Memorial Sloan-Kettering Cancer Center of New York City has found that while there are an estimated eight hundred thousand cases of skin cancer in America, that number could be reduced substantially if people would take simple precautions when exposed to direct sunlight.

Clearly Americans are prone to crisis management and fixing problems rather than working to prevent them before they occur. When in crisis we have incredible resolve to find solutions for our problems. Yet if we had the same resolve in regard to preventing those crises, we might avoid many trials and much pain.

This book is based on the self-evident truth, An ounce of prevention is worth a pound of cure. It's much easier to avoid making mistakes than it is to correct them after the fact. This is particularly true of parenting. Just ask any mother or father continually challenged by a contentious and rebellious teen: *Given a choice to start over, what would you do, work toward prevention or maintain the status quo and manage in crisis?*

While there are some individuals who make a living at counseling parents and teens in crisis, we personally find this approach frustrating. As we have listened through the years to angry accusations from both sides of the table (parents and teens), we have come to realize that many of the storms and stress experienced could have been minimized, if not prevented altogether, if these families had been given some practical guidance a few years earlier.

You now hold in your hands the guidebook we wish we could have given them. We are thankful that over the years, God has brought into our lives numerous people who have given us great insights regarding parenting. Perhaps the most important insight we have gained is this: *Rightly meeting the small challenges of the middle years significantly reduces the likelihood of big challenges in the teen years.* In other words, the groundwork you lay today will impact your relationship with your children long after they're grown. This book is as much about preventing serious teen/parent conflicts as it is about building a strong relationship with your middle-years child.

In this book, we will speak to you not only as teachers but as fellow parents. Though our children are now adults with their own children rapidly approaching the middle years, we remember clearly how we felt while parenting our children through this critical growth period, both where we failed and where we succeeded.

We say now, without hesitation, that the years when our kids were between the ages of eight and twelve were some of the most challenging for us as parents. Yes, even more challenging than the teen years! This is not because we weren't secure in our convictions or not desiring to honor God through our parenting. It is because there weren't a lot of Moms and Dads around who had set a standard, stuck by it, and could share with us practical advice about how we, too, could make the most of our children's preteen years.

Thankfully, we found the answers we were seeking, and now we want to share them with you. We want you not only to enjoy your child's preadolescent years and approach them with confidence, but to develop a positive view toward the potentially wonderful time to follow—the teen years. While we can offer you knowledge gained from our experience, only you can make the difference in your child's life.

Before we get started, there are two small matters of terminology to bring to your attention. First, when clinicians talk about pre-adolescence, or the preteen years, they are generally referring to children between the ages of ten and twelve. This book however, is broader in its scope and includes children who are eight and nine years old. This is because the hormonal changes experienced by preadolescents have actually begun by age eight. To stay consistent with contemporary terminology, we will use the words "preteen" when referring to ten- to twelve-year-old children but refer to the broader five year period, eight to twelve years of age, as the middle years.

Second, at times we used the masculine gender "he" when presenting examples and illustrations. This was done for our convenience. The principles presented, of course, apply equally to children of both genders.

We realize, just as you do, that there is a tremendous gap between the behavior, attitude, and maturity of an eight year old and that of a twelve year old. During these five years, boys and girls experience a tremendous amount of growth. However, children at both ends of this spectrum can share moral common ground. In the following pages, we'll show you how to instill in your child a moral maturity upon which he or she can build for a lifetime. Note that even though children of this age may share common ground, the principles we'll be sharing with you will be applied differently to different children, especially those of varying ages. Please take the information we give you and use it appropriately, according to where your child is developmentally.

And now, it's time to begin the process of growing together through the middle years. If we have learned anything from teaching frustrated parents battling their teenagers, it is this: The middle years, more than the teen years, are the crucible in which preparation for responsible living is established. The fifteen hundred days of preadolescence are all you have to prepare your kids for the nearly thirty-seven hundred days of adolescence.

Let's make the most of every minute!

Gary and Anne Marie
Los Angeles 1998

Chapter One

IF ONLY WE HAD KNOWN

The next time you're in a bookstore, check out the parenting section. Count all the books that prepare you for childbirth or your baby's first year of life. Next, visit the early childhood section and note the number of volumes available to help you through your child's critical toddler years. Move on to the teen section. There you will likely find a large number of books by a variety of experts discussing every adolescent issue, from bulimia to body piercing. Nearby in the general family section, you may find such titles as *The Vegetarian Child*, *Carbohydrate-Addicted Kids*, *Children with Work Inhibitions*, and *Children of Third Marriages*.

Now scan the different sections and try to find a book written about children living in the growth-packed years between the ages of eight and twelve. If your experience is like ours, you may want to ask the manager for help. We recently visited seven major book dealers within a three-mile radius of our home: a Super Crown Bookstore, two B. Dalton Bookstores, one Barnes and Noble, one Waldenbooks, and two Christian bookstores.

Yet, amazingly, out of all these stores, not one carried a single book written specifically about parenting a child through the middle years. The closest examples we could find were the few, but random, volumes of the Gesell Institute of Human

Development series by Dr. Louise Ames. Even these titles were limited to one year time periods of development.

Why such barrenness when it comes to the middle years? One possible explanation can be drawn from the character of our society. As we stated in the introduction, our society seems very willing to spend time and money to fix its problems, but very little of either to prevent them. In parenting, this is evidenced by the number of books written for the purpose of "fixing" America's teen problems after they occur.

Parents often find themselves struggling through their children's teen years, wondering: What could I have done to prevent the problems my family is now facing? Though a great number of families with teens find themselves in crisis, few Moms and Dads look to the five critical years between childhood and adolescence with much parental curiosity or concern. But they should.

ESTABLISHING A ROOT SYSTEM

Consider the example of the Chinese bamboo tree. Once the first sprout emerges from the soil, the rate of growth averages a little over two feet per day, culminating six weeks later in a ninety-foot tree. What is even more amazing is the root system that sustains and nurtures this explosive growth. From the time the seed is planted, it takes four years for an extensive network of roots to develop before the tender bamboo shoot ever breaks ground and heads for the sun.

This is a good analogy of what is happening with your middle-years child. The growth in these years is silent, extensive, and occurs mostly below the surface. Like the Chinese bamboo tree, your child is developing a supporting "root system" that will sustain and support him or her in the explosive growth years of adolescence. This is the time when you, the parent, must nurture, water, and tend the "seedling" in your care. We want to help prepare you to meet that challenge.

The middle years are perhaps the most significant attitude-forming ones in the life of a child. It is during this time that the roots of moral character are established. From the foundation that is formed, healthy or not-so-healthy family relationships will be built. These are the years when patterns of behavior are firmly established—patterns that will impact your parent/child relationship for decades to come. These are the years when growth takes place silently, deep within your middle-years child.

IN NEED OF PHILIP

In the truest sense, we started work on this book twenty-two years ago. That is when our children entered the middle years and when we first began to earnestly seek answers to our questions about parenting preadolescent children.

I (Gary) remember one Saturday afternoon in 1978 when as a young father, I reached a point of incredible frustration with our nine year old. My frustration was not over what she had done, but with our lack of wisdom about how to handle a recurring troublesome behavior.

Like many men, I tend to be action-oriented. I want to see the results of God's strategies (or at least what I think are God's strategies!) in the shortest period of time. In this particular case, I wanted to fix the problem with Amy and be done with it—forever. But I knew that wasn't going to happen because I didn't know what to do, or where to turn to find the answer. Not only were Anne Marie and I lacking short-term answers, we had no long-term plan to guide us in the future.

Yes, we were Christian parents. We knew the command of Proverbs 22:6: "Train up a child in the way he should go, and when he is old he will not depart from it." We knew Ephesians 6:4: "And you, fathers, do not provoke your children to wrath, but bring them up in the training and admonition of the Lord." We knew a dozen other verses related to parenting, but still we were despairing about the future.

Like the Ethiopian treasurer who needed Philip to help him understand the words written by the prophet Isaiah (Acts 8:30–31), we needed a teacher who could help us understand the complexities of parenting a middle-years child. We needed someone to show us how to be a proactive father or mother who would be there for the long haul. We needed the guidance of one who was sensitive to the expanding world of a nine-year-old child, and who could help us mature in biblical fatherhood or motherhood.

Ignorance is bliss, so says the proverb. This is true, however, only when a person remains oblivious to the fact that they are missing out on something important. A life of ignorance is not so blissful when we realize we're missing something crucial—but we don't know what it is. The awareness of need combined with the absence of knowledge can only breed frustration. That's what I sensed on that Saturday afternoon in 1978—a frustration born out of ignorance.

To some extent, at one time or another, all parents experience this type of frustration with their kids. They sense that they should be doing something to help their children mature and grow—but they don't know exactly what that something is. And while experiencing a certain level of frustration can help teach patience and the need for self-control, becoming overburdened with frustration only leads to a sense of despair and ongoing feelings of disappointment and guilt.

From these reoccurring feelings of disappointment and guilt often come the sinful strategies of relying upon excessive authority, power, and control. We parents may desire to respond biblically to our feelings, yet at the same time, it is natural for us to want to control something that seems out of control—especially when that something is our child.

Do you ever feel out of control with your middle-years child? We did. Our nine-year-old Amy was growing up too fast and claiming independence from our leadership too quickly. How much of this was the natural course of growing up, and how much of this was our failure to understand biblical fatherhood and motherhood? We did not know. But we did fear one thing—the future. If nine-year-old Amy rejected our guidance, what would life be like in a few short years when she became a teenager?

Many years have passed since that afternoon in 1978. By God's grace I did learn about fathering and Anne Marie learned about mothering. Over the years, we learned how to really love our kids, and the results were tangible, not only during our children's middle years, but in the years that followed. As a result of the foundation we laid during our children's preadolescent years, the subsequent teen years were the highlight of our parenting. Not only did we enjoy our children, more remarkably, our children really enjoyed us.

Now, after completing seven books and fifty-five videos on parenting, and with nearly twenty years of family ministry experience behind us, we can confidently tell you that close, intimate family relationships don't have to end shortly after kids hit adolescence. On the contrary, parents and children can establish a solid relational foundation that will see them through this potentially difficult stage of life, and the best time to do so is now: during the critically important middle years. As the parent of a middle-years son or daughter, you are in the ideal position to set the tone for your child's adolescence and to lay the foundation of future family harmony.

Today, you have an advantage that many parents of the previous generation did not: You have a place to turn for help. We have spent the last twenty years of our life preparing and providing help for parents because we remember when there was none. You can choose to take a positive, proactive approach to building a healthy relationship with your son or daughter right now. In the following chapters, we'll walk you through the process of building a strong, enduring parent/child relationship that can last a lifetime.

Where do you want your family to be in five or ten years? What are your hopes and desires for the future? What are your family goals? Are love, fun, harmony, peace, unity, and mutual adoration qualities for which your family is known? We hope so, but if not, we want to help you get to a place where they are, because these are the qualities that are indicative of healthy families. And a healthy family, Moms and Dads, is a great relational goal.

MARKS OF A HEALTHY FAMILY

What are the marks of a healthy family? Our ministry to parents has afforded us a better than average opportunity to observe and study the characteristics of healthy and not-so-healthy families. We have followed a number of the children in these families from highchair graduation to high school graduation. And while not every healthy family will exhibit all of the following characteristics, it is our experience that most strong families demonstrate a majority of these traits.

It is not uncommon for parents to believe either a family has these characteristics, or it doesn't. After years of study, it is our conclusion that healthy family relationships are cultivated, not inherited. This is a key concept to understand, because it means healthy family relationships are within your grasp.

Do you hear that, Mom and Dad? With God's grace, you *can* do it. We've done it. We personally know hundreds of parents—and know about thousands of others—who have done it. And now we're going to share with you the biblical principles we've learned and applied that make it possible.

Let's begin by taking a look at the ten positive characteristics of healthy families. The families we're talking about are not only healthy, they are healthy families *with teenagers*. Remember, this is where you're headed. There is great reason for hope for the teen years; these families are proof of it. As you're reading, think about whether these traits are common to your family today. If they're not, don't panic. You can get there. In fact, you should expect to get there before your child becomes a teen. Your family can and should be known for these characteristics—by the church and by the world.

CHARACTERISTICS COMMON TO HEALTHY FAMILIES

1. Healthy families have a core of shared values which all members embrace and to which all members submit.

What is family unity born of? Shared values. Do not think for a moment that you can have peace in the family if your children's core values are in conflict with yours. Nothing outside the family can produce social order better than shared values within the family. Can a family live peaceably if individual members differently interpret the meaning of honesty, kindness, generosity, truthfulness, respect, honor, obedience, fairness, or friendship? Certainly not. Anarchy and endless wars will follow if everyone does what is right in his or her own eyes. That is why family life that is established on a weak moral foundation is threatened from the start. You cannot find the basis for unity or hope in a healthy family apart from shared values.

2. Healthy families know how to communicate with each other.

Good communication is not just about transmitting facts or giving commands such as "Take the garbage out now." It is about sharing feelings and emotions. When our girls reached the ages of ten and eleven, and in the years that followed, we talked together far more than we ever had before. These talk times happened throughout the day, but particularly at dinner and bedtime. You, too, must give your children time to talk and to communicate. And you must share a part of yourself with them as well. This is an important part of growing relationally with your kids.

3. Healthy families have parents who are not afraid to say "I was wrong."

As parents, we need to understand that when we make a mistake it's not only acceptable, it's important that we say to our children, "I was wrong. Will you forgive me?" Our kids already know we're not perfect; we're not hiding anything from them by not admitting it. It means a great deal to them, especially during the middle years, when we acknowledge our errors. If you say to your three year old, "I was wrong," the concept doesn't stick. At this age children still believe Mom and Dad are perfect. But when your kids reach the middle years, there's an awakening to the possibility that Mom and Dad are fallible. Your words, "I was wrong; I'm sorry; Will you forgive me?" produce a healthy vulnerability that will bring your child closer to you. He or she will know there's no wall between you; Mom and Dad are not hiding behind the pretense of perfection.

4. Healthy families maintain the marriage as a recognized priority of family health.

Except for some extreme circles within feminism, the belief that healthy marriages make for healthy families is still popular with clinicians from every background and school of thought. Every child longs for the security that a healthy marriage brings to the family, and that desire to know Mom and

Dad love each other does not diminish over time. The husband/wife relationship is the first social relationship established in Scripture, and for good reason. All other relationships within the family are dependent upon the healthy alliance of the husband and wife. The quality of the mother/child–father/child relationship depends on the quality of the husband/wife relationship.

5. Healthy families make time to be with each other and to attend each others events.
Cultivate your sense of family identity. Give each other time. If you don't have the time, make the time. Once your child becomes a teenager, and particularly after he or she gets a driver's license, it will be even easier for everyone to scatter in different directions. You must set a precedent now. The family must schedule time to come together and recharge their relational "batteries."

6. Healthy families have teens who are confident of their parents' trust in them.
You are now at a point where your children want to know, Do Mom and Dad trust me? When we surveyed one hundred ninth- through twelfth-graders for our *Reaching the Heart of Your Teen* series, these teens told us that what would motivate them the most, what would hold them close to the family, is knowing Mom and Dad trusted them. Lack of trust can become a genesis of conflict. It's important that you give your children opportunities to prove themselves trustworthy.

7. Healthy families have members who are loyal to each other.
By this time, your family has already gone through difficulties and good times together. You should already see signs of loyalty being demonstrated. An example of this may be you

coming to bat for them during times of trouble, or an older child coming alongside a younger sibling at school.

8. Healthy families choose conflict resolution over conflict avoidance.
Healthy families know how to resolve conflict and choose to do so, rather than avoiding or running from it. Strong family relationships require mutual respect and the freedom for each member to go to another and deal with interpersonal issues. When we avoid conflict or a situation that puts us at odds with people we love and by whom we want to be loved, we do so out of a fear of not being loved, appreciated, or understood. But running from a problem, or attempting to avoid it, breeds frustration, resentment, and bitterness. We strengthen our relationships not by avoiding conflicts, but by knowing how to lovingly resolve them.

9. Healthy families have a corporate sense of responsibility to all members.
A corporate sense of responsibility is about more than just loyalty, which is an emotion. It involves actions: the choice to commit and the decision to follow through on that commitment to the family unit. This is characterized by a visible demonstration of responsible behavior; in response to a need, everyone pitches in and helps.

10. Healthy families swap family rules for family courtesies as the child matures.
Young children live by rules, but by the time they hit their early teen years moral requirements should be swapped for moral courtesies. This means rules that were once adhered to because the child yielded to the power of your authority are now adhered to because the value behind the rule is understood and internalized. The teen now does right because it is

the right thing to do, not because failure to comply will bring punishment.

Families who share these characteristics are blessed, indeed. However, it's important that you not assume healthy families are without problems. This is not the case. Stress, trials, conflicts, financial problems, and sinful attitudes confront healthy families as much as they do unhealthy ones. The difference is this: Healthy families know how to deal with stress; they know how to draw upon each other's strengths to get through their trials; they know how to resolve conflict instead of avoiding it; they know how to confess their faults to one another. Soon you will know these things too.

THE MIDDLE-YEARS TEST

Now that we have looked at the traits of healthy families, let's check the pulse of yours. The following questions are designed to help you determine where you are today and how you can improve.

Take the test for each middle-years child in your household. The scoring summary found at the conclusion of the test represents responses from many of the healthy families we have worked with over the years.

Please note, we designed this test to provide you with an objective point of reference, not to serve as a definitive judgment on your family's state of health. The results are significant only as far as they impact your ability to parent more effectively. Your final score will help you evaluate where you stand in comparison to the hundreds of families who formed the basis of this test. The test is not meant to encourage or discourage you; its purpose is simply to provide a starting point from which you can begin working toward improvement.

No one needs to see your score, so please consider each question carefully. Honestly evaluate the overall characterization of your preteen's behavior before marking down your answer. We challenge you to this level of integrity for your family's sake.

This test is divided into two sections, each with a different rating scale. Please note the difference when you go to the second section. After completing both sections, add the scores, and record the total below in the space provided. If for some reason you don't know the answer to a question, make an educated guess.

Section One

Writing in your responses adjacent to each question in this section, rate the questions using a 1 to 5 scale.

1 = This is very representative of our child or our relationship.

2 = This is usually representative of our child or our relationship.

3 = Sometimes this is true of our child or our relationship, but just as often it is not.

4 = This is not usually true of our child or our relationship.

5 = This rarely, if ever, is true of our child or our relationship.

1. ____If our preadolescent was at a neighbor's house and there was a questionable television program or movie on, he/she would either call home to find out if it was ok to watch it or would make a decision not to watch the program.

2. ____Our preadolescent is characterized by self-generated initiative, meaning that when our child sees something that needs to be done, he/she does it.

3. ____Our preadolescent is characterized by the same level of behavior outside our presence as when he/she is with us.

4. ____If our preadolescent has been in trouble while away

from us, he/she will come and tell us before we find out from someone else.

5. ____Our preadolescent is beginning to pursue his/her own relationship with God.

6. ____If our preadolescent sees a piece of paper on the floor, even if he/she didn't drop it he/she will be characterized by picking it up.

7. ____ At this age our preadolescent knows the moral reason behind most instructions we give.

8. ____Our preadolescent is characterized by coming to us in humility if he/she thinks our instructions are unfair.

9. ____Our preadolescent considers his/her siblings as part of his/her inner circle of best friends.

10. ____For his/her age, our preadolescent has enough sense to avoid troubling situations by his/her own initiative.

11. ____Our preadolescent looks forward to special times with only the family.

12. ____Our preadolescent can accept "no" for an answer without blowing up.

13. ____Our preadolescent knows that if we wrong him/her in any way, he/she can count on an apology from us.

14. ____Our preadolescent picks up after himself/herself.

15. ____In our family, we practice seeking forgiveness from one another rather than just saying "I'm sorry."

Now add up all of the numbers you placed in the blanks above and enter the total score in the blank below.

Section One Score _____

Section Two

Writing in your responses on the blanks adjacent to each question in this section, rate the questions using a 5 to 1 scale.

5=Always true, or this is very representative of our child, his/her feelings, our feelings, or our relationship.

4=Often the case, or this is usually representative of our child, his/her feelings, our feelings, or our relationship.

3=Sometimes this is true but just as often it is not.

2=This happens, but not often. Or, this is not usually representative of our child, his/her feelings, our feelings, or our relationship.

1=This is rarely, if ever, true of our child or our relationship.

1. ____Our preadolescent seems to have a split personality. He/she acts one way when he/she is with us, but is not as yielding to authority when at school or church.

2. ____Our preadolescent is jealous and pouts when something good happens to a sibling but does not happen to him/her.

3. ____We seem to be tightening the boundaries rather than loosening them now that our child is in the middle years.

4. ____We are beginning to notice that our child's attitudes are more greatly impacted by the negative influence of peers than by the positive influence of family.

5. ____We are always reminding our preadolescent to pick up after himself/herself.

6. ____When we ask our preadolescent to do something we always end up in a power struggle.

7. ____Worldly, trendy fashions are becoming a source of conflict between our preadolescent and us.

8. ____Our preadolescent seems to frequently take advantage of siblings.

9. ____Our preadolescent gets angry when things don't go his/her way.

10. ____Our preadolescent seems to make impetuous decisions without thought of future consequences.

11. ____Our preadolescent will do something good to get out of doing what he/she was told.

12. ____Our preadolescent will tell us a partial truth or openly lie to us rather than admit irresponsibility.

13. ____Our preadolescent is never satisfied with just "no." He/she always has to ask a series of challenging "whys."

14. ____Even if we were just going next door, I don't think we could trust leaving our preadolescent alone for an hour.

15. ____Our preadolescent tends to be drawn to the kids who are always getting in trouble rather than the good kids who stay out of trouble.

Section Two Score_____

Section One Score _____

Grand Total _____

Compare your score to the numbers posted under the Middle Years Healthy Family Profile Summary.

MIDDLE-YEARS HEALTHY FAMILY PROFILE SUMMARY

30-45=Healthy, right on track, need to fine tune some issues.

46-60=Healthy, basically on track, working on some issues.

61-75=There are a number of behavioral concerns that if not corrected now, can lead to struggles and conflict during adolescence.

76-90=There are many negative patterns signaling that course correction is needed immediately.

91-150=Off course.

Name of child _____   Score _____

Name of child _____   Score _____

How did you do on your middle-years test? By identifying your child's character strengths and weaknesses now, you have gained a great advantage in parenting. You can now work objectively toward encouraging and reinforcing the positive aspects of your child's character while shoring up the weak ones. You can give focused attention to exact needs as you work to bring your child to maturity.

But even with this advantage, please accept the fact all parents must face; our children—and we, as parents—will never be perfect. Nor will our children's teen years be perfect. These years can be great, but not flawless. Regardless of how many books we read, how many seminars we attend, how many classes we take, or how many self-evaluating tests we fill out, we're not going to be perfect people until we get to heaven.

That last statement should be liberating and encouraging, not limiting or discouraging. It implies this truth: we do not have to be in perfect mastery at every phase of our children's development. That is where the grace of God comes in—if we let it. When we are weak He is strong.

BRINGING IT HOME

Regardless of how you scored on the test above, take time now to discuss the results with your spouse, and if you think it appropriate, your children. This evaluation is not all-conclusive but does serve as an indicator of the strengths and weaknesses of your family. Your score reflects what is going on in your family today. Now you have a starting point. Take time to share your answers to the question: Where do we want to be in a few years? Through discussion, begin to build a shared vision for what your family relationships will look like in the future.

Chapter Two

COMING AND GOING: THE MIDDLE-YEARS TRANSITION

A t a recent conference a frazzled mother confessed to us and to our audience: "My children bring out the worst in me."

"Yes," we responded. "That's exactly what children do to parents. They expose us for who we are and what we know. They also expose us for who we're not, and what we don't know." We all know that parenting is a process that leads to maturity. This is true, however, not only of our children's maturity, but *our* maturity. Marriage is blessed not solely because it produces children; rather, children themselves are part of the blessing. They are an important factor in the process God uses to produce two mature beings: Mom and Dad.

Consider God's moral law. This can be defined biblically as a prescription for daily moral living that reflects the will and character of God. Every day our children test not only our moral knowledge, but our moral fortitude. Their need for guidance forces us to learn about God's teachings concerning right and wrong. For example, we learn about patience because our children require so much of it. They teach us verbal self-control because godly parenting cannot be explosive, critical, or sarcastic. In this way, our children reveal the strongholds of our sin and our areas of weakness where God can make us strong.

Every major teaching basic to the Christian faith—love, mercy, grace, justice, repentance, forgiveness, restoration, compassion, patience, and self-control, to name a few—is challenged daily in parenting. God uses the parenting process to bring moms and dads to maturity in a way no other life experience can. It provides ideal circumstances in which we can learn, for no one else in the world will be as forgiving of our shortcomings as our own children. God uses our middle-years children to help us mature, and to hold us accountable before Him.

As parents, we can't completely avoid making mistakes. But we can become students of our children and do our best to make wise decisions regarding their upbringing. This is where we should invest our energy. It is impossible to relive yesterday's missed opportunities or to predict what tomorrow holds. Hope for the future lies in living each day as it comes, rather than regretting the past or living in fearful anticipation of the future.

One way to reduce parenting apprehension is to learn what you can expect in the years ahead. Like animals, humans follow a pattern of development. Because of this, we can predict what goes on during certain phases of the growth process. The middle-years transition period is no exception.

MIDDLE-YEARS TRANSITION: ARRIVALS AND DEPARTURES

There is not a major airport in the United States through which we have not passed at least once. Forty-two weeks a year, we travel from our home in California to other cities throughout the world to lead parenting seminars. We understand the potential difficulties associated with fixed airline schedules. We know what it is like to arrive from one city, deplane, rush to find the next gate, and be off again.

The airlines also know the potential for passengers to lose their way while in transit. That is why they have uniformed agents standing at the door, or waiting at the gate area, to help deplaning passengers in need of connecting flight information. These agents direct passengers from where they are to where they need to be.

During your child's middle years, one of your primary functions as Mom or Dad is to play the role of gate agent. As your child arrives from a wide range of childhood experiences, your job is to point him or her in the right direction, and in some cases, to lead the way. This means that you yourself must have an clear picture of where your child is headed.

At eight years of age, an intriguing growth period begins. This is because children at this stage arrive from so many developmental directions. Between the ages of nine and eleven they are making numerous transitions—from where they have been developmentally to where they are going. By the age of twelve, most children are ready to take off again and head toward a place called "adolescence and maturity."

Each of the transitions listed below is an important connection in your child's journey to the teen years. Your job as gate agent is to help guide your middle-years child from where he has come to where he must go. This process starts with the knowledge of change. What should you expect? Here are seven critical transitions to ponder.

Transition One:
From Childhood and Childhood Structures

The middle years are a time when children start the long process of metamorphosis—moving away from childhood structures, dependencies, and interests—toward healthy independence. During this time, there is a shift from a world centered largely around relationships with Mom, Dad, and siblings, to a world in which relationships with peers, friends, and hero figures begin to draw greater focus.

At eight or nine, your child has already done an enormous amount of learning. Contrast him or her with the near to helpless toddler of a few years ago who needed the structure of Mom and Dad's direct companionship, love, and supervision. Wake time, nap time, mealtime, and playtime were all orchestrated by a guiding parent. Your child's friends were limited to the kids in the nursery, Sunday school, or his or her weekday play groups. Your son or daughter lived in a world that was predominately structured and made secure by you.

Consider the child who, at five, walked with you to the bus stop everyday, or who at six, advanced to crossing the street by him- or herself. Now your child is notably less dependent on you and the sheltering structures that were created for his or her protection (and your comfort). Your preadolescent's long-standing preoccupation with personal caretakers will be replaced by a driving sense of his or her own self-sufficiency.

This particular transition is demonstrated by the way a child attempts to distance himself from early childhood structures. While such language didn't bother the child at age five or six, at eight or nine years old that same boy or girl will object to conversations that describe him or her in childhood terms, such as, "He's my little guy," or "Yes, she's my princess." Gary remembers how, at eight years old, he heard his mother exclaim unashamedly to his second grade teacher: "Yes, Gary, is my baby." He had heard that phrase a hundred times before. But this time he was so embarrassed by her declaration, he didn't want to go to school the next day. That experience was a signal that he had arrived at a new phase and realization: *I may still be a kid, but I'm not a little kid anymore. So please, Mom, don't tell people I'm your baby.* These are real emotions for the middle-years child. Being aware of them will help make this particular transition easier for you both. You went through these feelings, and so will your son or daughter.

Early in the middle-years transition, children also begin to reject minor childhood-related associations that he or she previously found comforting. The little girl who once was consoled after an injury by sitting on Mom's lap may start going to her siblings for comfort. The young boy who would not go anywhere without his stuffed animal, now buries it in his toy box. Or the son who, at six, found comfort in walking with his mother on the first day of school, prefers, at eight, that she wave good-bye from the porch while he heads off to class with his friends.

Making adjustments and finding relational equilibrium with maturing children is one of the more difficult tasks of parenthood. But by the end of this growth period, a healthy restructuring of relationships will have occurred for both you and your child.

Transition Two: To Knowing the Facts

This middle-years transition involves your child's ability to relate to other children as peers and other adults as something more than parental substitutes. Boys and girls of this period demonstrate a need to organize, categorize, and play by the rules. It is important to them that they get their facts right (although during this phase they have an oversimplified notion of the correctness of their own assessment). Have you ever watched or listened to a group of eight-year-old boys play baseball?

"You're out! I touched the base."

"No, I'm not! You have to touch *me*."

They can barely swing the bat, but they brandish their

knowledge of the rules as if they had a deep and abiding understanding of them.

Or perhaps you're having a conversation with another adult in which you describe an incident that occurred at the market today. The only other eye-witness to the event, your nine-year-old daughter, takes it upon herself to make sure you get the facts right. That's when you hear, "No, Mom, that's not how it happened. The man with the shopping cart bumped the manager and then..."

Do not be surprised when your attempt to abbreviate a conversation is met by a challenge from your middle-years child who seems to have, all of a sudden, a desperate need to set the record straight.

Add birth order to this mix. Because the eldest is born into a world of adults and not siblings, she tends to have an increased need to be "right" about all things. If another child or sibling breaks the rules, she is relentless in her efforts to straighten that child out. Look for these verbal declarations— they're all part of the transition process.

Transition Three: From Imagination to Reason

With the middle years comes a distinct shift toward logical thinking and a new capacity for moral understanding. These are the two prerequisites necessary for your child to regulate his or her own behavior in the future. Logic and reason now help him or her to begin overcoming and replacing the issues of life that are unknown or left to the imagination.

Think about how children deal with fear of the unknown or unexplained circumstances. Because younger children's imaginations develop more rapidly than their reasoning skills, these kids often exaggerate the dangers of fear-provoking situations.

Gary remembers the day he, a bike-riding six-year-old, turned his brother's red Schwinn up the street to a friend's house. Because he was paying more attention to the forest and fields on either side of the road than he was to the pathway in front of him, he did not see the small branch lying on the roadway, directly in his path. At the last moment, the piece of wood caught his eye. With no time to swerve, he made a split-second decision to ride over it—dead center. As he approached it, he knew something was wrong. But the sense of fear did not overtake him until the left side of the branch, freed from the weight of his front tire, rose up with a violent jerk and hissed. Gary had run over a three-foot snake!

Gary survived the fright of that afternoon and even forgot about it by bedtime. But in the middle of the night, with the wind howling through the trees outside his window, Gary woke with a start. As he surveyed his room, among the dancing moonlight shadows he saw something lying curled up at the far end of his bed. It didn't move, but he knew the thing was looking right at him. The snake he had run over earlier in the day—it was there, in his bedroom, on his bed! Somehow it had found him. How did it get into the house? Gary wondered. Oh, yes! The basement window! His dad always kept it open a little.

Gary studied the creature. Would it move if he moved? He knew that no matter what, Mr. Snake had him trapped. There was only one thing he could do: keep his eye on that curled up thing and watch if it moved any closer. And that's what Gary tried to do, although eventually, he fell asleep.

The next morning, Gary awoke to find that comforting light had replaced the moonlit shadows…and his curled up leather belt had replaced the snake.

This story clearly demonstrates how imagination influences a young child's perception of reality. During the middle years, however, this influence begins to change. One of the great transitions realized by middle-years children is the awakening of reason over fearful imagination. This means your eight year old will begin to appear more daring and adventuresome and less restrained by fear of the unknown.

Transition Four:
To New Emotional Patterns and Expressions

Human emotions are the common link of humanity. Every child comes into this life with the potential of experiencing the full range of emotions. Happiness and sadness, joy and sorrow, hatred and love are but a few examples. Obviously, these emotions influence the way we think and act.

Though God grants the same emotions to all of humanity, each of us can respond to these feelings in a variety of ways. Some responses are constructive; others detrimental to our well-being. In other words, it is not the emotions themselves that get us into trouble, but the manner in which we deal with them.

Interestingly, the more often an emotional response is experienced, the greater the likelihood that it will develop into a habit. Developing positive habits is particularly important during the middle years, because this is the season of life in which a child's moral knowledge (moral truth taught by parents and teachers), combined with his or her emotions, can help to establish patterns of right behavior.

For example, the child who learns early in life that "a soft answer turns away wrath" (Proverbs 15:1a) or "vengeance is mine, I will repay, says the Lord" (Romans 12:19) is likely to carry these teachings into adulthood. Your four year old can memorize these verses, but your eight year old can understand and start to routinely act upon them.

Do not miss this important point: Especially during the

middle years, you and your home environment will play a dominant role in shaping your child's profile of emotional responses. If right responses are not learned during the middle years, the teen years will most likely be characterized by wrong ones.

The middle years also bring about a shift in the outward expression of emotions. A young child's emotional outbursts last a few minutes, then they are over. Contrast this response with that of the socially-sensitive middle-years child whose short-lived outbursts have been exchanged for drawn-out periods of moodiness.

What all this demonstrates is that your middle-years son or daughter can now exercise cognitive control over express-ing his or her emotions. A few years earlier, this was not the case. The decision of how to behave is your son or daughter's; however, you still play a significant role in shaping how your child develops his or her responses. We urge you to take advantage of this natural learning curve.

Transition Five: To Hormone-Activated Bodies

It is widely believed that hormonal changes begin just as a child reaches the teen years, and that these naturally set into motion a series of defiant acts and rebellious mood swings. Yet it is a fact that hormonal changes in the endocrine system begin in children at approximately age seven, not twelve or thirteen, as commonly believed. You may have already begun to see the effects. Perhaps you have even found yourself thinking, "My child is only eight or nine. It can't be hormones yet."

But it is. Yes, Mom and Dad, your middle-years child is hormonally active. From this point on, he or she will experi-ence greater emotional highs and lows. This may, in turn, affect behavior. But the fact that your child is undergoing these changes does not provide an excuse for wrong behavior.

Have you ever wondered why your nine-year-old daughter can, in a cyclical way, change moods overnight, sometimes becoming emotionally irrational? She may go through cycles of discouragement, breaking out in tears over minor details. Her face becomes a little more oily and she is sure everyone is noticing. For a few days she becomes more snippety toward her siblings. Then just as quickly, she returns to being the stable child you once knew. Hormones are at work.

While hormones play their part, the moral environment in which your child is raised also plays a significant role in shaping the perception of his or her changing body and the sexual tension natural to growth. Clinicians have noted that children who come from differing moral home climates will have very different sensual experiences. For example, young girls weaned on MTV are more likely to direct their budding sense of womanhood toward images similar to those promoted by the sexual image makers of MTV. In contrast, pubescent daughters coming from homes that do not allow such degrading influences, tend to direct their budding sexual awareness into channels of innocent romantic thought.

Have your ever watched *Anne of Green Gables* and *Anne of Avonlea*? It took Anne, the main character of this drama, eight hours (in real time and eight years in story time) to realize it was Gilbert, her old school chum, she really loved.

While such romantic portrayals are entertaining for a sixty-year-old woman, and perhaps confusing for a six-year-old girl, the ten-year-old girl sitting on the couch enters into eight hours of romance by identifying herself with the heroine. Why is she hooked, but not her six-year-old female cousin or her eleven-year-old brother? Because hormones active in her body have brought about a budding sense of romance. Her body awakens her mind to a vague but real awareness that someday, there will be a Gilbert in her life.

Endocrine changes awake a sense of romantic sensitivity in girls much sooner than they do in boys. Your ten-year-old daughter is asking: "Mom, how did you and Dad meet?" or "Where did you go on your first date?" Meanwhile, a boy of the same age is asking, "Mom, have you seen my football?"

While thoughts of romance and images of knights-in-shining-armor dance in your daughter's head, it will be another year or two before the neighbor boy of the same age begins to think of your daughter as something more than a good right fielder or someone to torment with his pet rat. But in time, preteen boys, too, succumb to the powerful effect hormones have on their views of the opposite sex.

Transition Six:
To the Growing Influence of Peers

Hormones directly affect a child's body chemistry. In doing so, they also affect the child's view of self and his or her standing within the group. The middle years are marked by a greater sensitivity to the differences between self and peers. Any slight deviation in growth, or secondary sex characteristics that differ from those of the group, will cause the middle-years child to measure him-or herself by what is considered "normal" among peers.

Such an occurrence is natural, unavoidable, and to be expected. The young girl who begins to develop prematurely will measure herself against other girls. The boy who starts to show hairs on his chin, or who begins to grow disproportionally in height, becomes self-consciousness of his differences.

This awareness leads to a growing interest in the opinions of others in a child's peer group. He or she asks: What is the group wearing, listening to, doing? Where are they going?

And what does all this mean to me? A fuller discussion of peer involvement, relationships, and influence will occur in chapter 6. For now, it is enough to say the effects of this transition will be felt for quite some time.

Transition Seven:
To a Sense of Morality

Of all the transitions listed, this one will receive the most attention in this book. We believe biblical morality is the only foundation upon which healthy relationships are forged and strong families built. Only when we know how to rightly relate with one another can we even think about getting along with others in our family and community.

Because the middle years are typically far less traumatic than the "terrible twos" or the tumultuous teen years, parents tend not to have a sense of moral urgency. Yet, if there ever was a time of ripening when a child seeks moral knowledge, it is during these precious middle years. This is the time when you as a parent can encourage the development of moral consciousness in your child.

During the middle years, children not only understand the wider scope of moral truth, they can begin to use it to regulate their lives. Soon they will be able to conform their outward behavior voluntarily, apart from the fear of reproof that so often accompanies a younger child's moral decision-making process. Remember the bamboo tree of chapter 1, with its extensive root system? The middle years is the time when your child will strike deep moral roots—with or without your moral guidance.

Young children live off of Mom and Dad's values. The middle-years transition, however, brings kids to the place where they begin to take personal ownership of their values. Are you ready to help your child make the transition? We'll explain in upcoming chapters just how you will guide that process.

SUMMARY

The middle years is a time of realignment and sometimes course correction for children and parents. These are transition years when children start the long process of metamorphosis—moving away from childhood dependencies and interests, toward healthy independence and self-responsibility. It is a period marked by a greater sensitivity to the differences between self and peers and thus a growing interest in peer approval which can lead to peer pressure.

The endocrine system begins to release potent hormones nudging boys and girls to sexual awareness. Now, boys and girls begin to change their minds about the opposite sex and start, all of a sudden, to view the other gender as attractive. Your son or daughter will begin to pay more attention to physical hygiene and personal grooming, including hairstyles and dress.

The middle years are a time of great moral and intellectual growth, when your child will begin to take ownership of his or her values and beliefs. It is a time when the world opens up to them and when the meaning of life beyond Mom and Dad's design begins to take shape. Yes, it is a time of great transition for your child—and for you.

BRINGING IT HOME

1. In chapter 1, we used the analogy of the Chinese bamboo tree to illustrate the growth and development that children experience during the middle years. In your own words, explain this analogy.

2. In chapter 1, we also introduced a list of ten traits common to healthy families. Review the list again. Identify two

traits about which you feel fairly secure and two traits on which, as a family, feel you need to work.

3. In this chapter we used the example of a uniformed gate agent to illustrate an important goal of middle-years parenting. Sum up your understanding of how you are like a "gate agent" in your child's life.

4. How might your family's moral environment help shape your child's perception of his or her changing body and the sexual tension naturally felt during this growth phase?

5. Describe in your own words the middle-years transition that occurs in relation to morality.

Chapter Three

JUST AHEAD: ADOLESCENCE AND MATURITY

Man is a builder. The Bible illustrates this trait. In the first book of the Old Testament, we learn that Cain, after being driven from the face of God, went to the land of Nod and built a city (Genesis 4:16–17). Years later, Nimrod, a descendent of Noah, built another city in the land of Shinar with a tower that extended to heaven (Genesis 10:10; 11:4). Jesus and the apostles used the words *building* and *builders* in many of their stories to drive home spiritual truth (Matthew 7:24; Mark 12:10; Luke 12:18, 14:28; Acts 7:49; Hebrews 11:10; 1 Peter 2:5). One reason the "building" metaphor is common in Scripture is because mankind can so easily relate to it.

Most of us would not attempt to build a house without blueprints. Even with blueprints, we would not build the roof without first knowing how to build the supporting structure. Having worked in new home construction, I (Gary) know firsthand the pain and aggravation of having to tear work down and start over because someone missed a construction code, or a door or window was framed an inch too narrow. Starting over is as much discouraging as it is difficult. As the workers undid the wrong, they were constantly reminded of their human shortcomings.

During the process of building their family, parents often find that they have to "tear down walls" and start over when their kids hit the teen years. In part, the problems that occur are the result of a lack of direction and foresight. Parents have no blueprint to measure the accuracy of their progress. Some sit back and let the teen years simply "happen" to them rather than choosing to be a proactive project foreman.

This chapter offers a blueprint for the future: a point of reference to provide guidance for the middle years. You will better understand and relate to your middle-years child after you gain a working knowledge of where you're going and what the finished product looks like.

THE GOAL: ADOLESCENT MATURITY

Your child has now reached the middle years. This is a time not for ambivalence, but for vision. In a few years, your son or daughter is going to step into adolescence. How should you prepare yourselves as parents? We suggest starting out with a right perspective of this period.

Forget everything you've heard about the tortuous teenage years. Put aside all thoughts about unavoidable rebellion, emotional withdrawal, and communication breakdowns. Block out the mental images of your son or daughter's transformation from loving child to angry, resentful adolescent. These are the stereotypes society has led you to expect, but such hope-draining predictions don't have to come true for you and your family. You *can* have great teens and great teen years. Successful parenting is not simply a matter of chance. But a certain amount of foresight is necessary if you want a healthy outcome for your child's preteen and teen years.

If adolescent maturity is the goal of our efforts to parent children through the middle years (and it is), then the following questions must be answered: What is adolescence? What is maturity? What does maturity look like? When is it achieved? What are the components of maturity? Do all children go through adolescence and arrive at maturity at the same rate and time? What roles do Mom and Dad play? What are the variables involved? In this chapter, we will examine these important matters related to adolescence and maturity, as well as the role of parental authority.

DEFINING TERMS

For every human "grown-up," there was a period of eight or nine years when he or she was no longer a child but not yet an adult. The terms used to designate an individual in this in-between period of life include *adolescent, teen,* and *youth.*

Derived from the Latin verb *adolescere,* adolescence means to ripen or grow into maturity. The word "teen" (or "teenager") is derived from the numerical age span of thirteen to nineteen years. The Bible doesn't use the terms "adolescent" or "teenager," but refers to children of this approximate age as *youth* or *young men.* Daniel, Shadrach, Meshach, and Abed-Nego were all "young men" when taken to Babylon to serve Nebuchadnezzar (Daniel 1:3–4). Bible scholars place their ages between twelve and fifteen years. Regardless of which term is used, each of these words represents essentially the same period of growth and development in the context of our society.

Noah Webster defined maturity as "a state of full growth." What does that look like today? In our society, maturity is understood and marked by a person's point of entry into the adult community. Full maturity is reached through a combination of biological growth, legal considerations, societal dictates, and parental expectations. These four categories not only define maturity for us, they give meaning to the period of adolescence.

Physical Maturity

Adolescence is the time when children ripen into physical maturity. Because all humans follow the same patterns of physical growth and development, physical maturation is reached at approximately the same time: eighteen to twenty years of age. This is when a child achieves maximum body growth (height) and when the ossification of the sacral bones takes place, and thus the skeletal growth process ends.

Legal Maturity

Adolescence is also the time when children ripen into legal maturity. When we say someone has reached the age of legal maturity, we mean the person is old enough to participate in the full range of adult behavior permitted by law. Every nation determines its own legal customs and timetable for allowing an individual passage into the adult community.

In our society, legal rights are granted to an individual gradually until the fullness of legal maturity is reached at the age of twenty-one. While a sixteen year old is granted the legal right to drive a car, he legally cannot serve in the military or vote in a public election until he is eighteen. Our society has determined that the age of twenty-one is the legal entry point into the adult community, at which point a young person is responsible for his actions and can be held accountable in a court of law.

Social and Intellectual Maturity

Adolescence is the time when children ripen into social and intellectual maturity. Social maturity, as used in this context, refers to one's readiness to participate in social policy that affects public welfare and the mutual good of the society at large. Intellectual maturity refers to the minimum level of intellectual and academic attainment necessary to function in the adult community.

Every society sets its own minimum social and intellectual standards that must be met before a person is accepted as an adult. The very complexity of American adult life demands that our children transition into a period of adolescent ripening before entering the adult world. In our society, the social and intellectual entrance into the adult community is realized at approximately twenty-one years old.

Moral Maturity

Adolescence is the time when children ripen into moral maturity. It is natural to think that moral maturity follows the same growth pattern as does legal, physical, social, and intellectual maturity. You may assume that since a child tends to mature in each of these categories just before entrance to adulthood, personal morality follows suit. Not so. Unfortunately, such thinking can cause parents to lose a sense of urgency. This will result in delayed moral maturity in their children.

In a biblical context, moral maturity (which we defined in chapter 2 as "thinking and acting in harmony with God's moral law") should show itself between the ages of thirteen and fifteen. This is when children become sons and daughters of God's moral law. In the Hebrew economy of the Old Testament, the Jewish bar mitzvah served this purpose for boys. By ceremony, it marked the age of moral responsibility when a youth became accountable to God for his actions.

Too often, parents of preadolescents misjudge the timing of a child's moral ripening. They view the teen years as the period in which great moral *learning* takes place rather than the time when moral *behavior* should already be realized. During the critical middle years, your child has a great ability to understand and experience the greatness of God's moral truth. This is the period when your son or daughter can choose to make your values his or her own.

In future chapters we'll discuss more about the elements

of training. But for now, let's look at the relationship between moral maturity and the use of parental authority: specifically, how not to abuse it.

LESS IS MORE

Now that your child is in the middle years, it's time to ask yourself: Am I using more or less of my authority to bring about moral conformity? Consider carefully your answer to this question. While many parents feel tempted to exert greater control during the middle and teen years, we want to stress that *you must begin to rely less upon the power of your authority*. As your preteen approaches adolescence, the need for your parental rule should decline in direct proportion to his or her increased rate of moral self-rule.

The middle years are a potentially confusing time not just for your child, but also for you as a parent. Changes are occurring within your son or daughter, yet you're not entirely sure what is happening. Like many Moms and Dads, you may fear the unknown. You may feel anxious about what lies ahead. This apprehension can spark a desire to increase your control. At times you may feel that the best way to manage the future is to bring in the boundaries to more fully control your preteen.

Or, perhaps you may go to the other extreme and completely surrender, saying: "There's nothing I can do. During the teen years, my child is going to do whatever he wants to do." As the teen years draw near, you find yourself pulled into the despair felt by so many parents in our society.

Nowhere is there greater confusion than around the stormy topic of parental control and use of authority. It seems that unnecessary controversy has replaced common sense. The permissive parent looks at the authoritarian parent and says: "I don't want to be like *that* Mother and Father. They're too strict!" Meanwhile, the authoritarian parent looks at the permissive household and says, "I don't want my children acting like *that*. Those kids are out of control!" The permissive parent who controls too little and the authoritarian parent who controls too much both deprive their children of basic skills necessary for healthy adolescence. Too often these kids hit the teen years either under-directed or under-motivated.

You have another choice. You don't have to increase your control at this stage of the game, nor do you have to back away from your authority. As you approach your child's teen years, you can transition from relying upon the power of your authority to tapping into the power of your relational influence. This is the one great transition every parent must make.

THE AUTHORITY EXCHANGE

Mankind has always struggled with authority. But authority is absolutely essential because law and order for the family and society are dependent on its proper administration. In the Christian family, the Bible not only provides the basis of all authority, but also the ethics that govern how it should be used. Like the character of love (1 Corinthians 13:4–7), biblical authority is full of integrity, gentle, consistent and gracious; it is not presumptuous, proud, unkind, or unfair. Biblical authority is motivated by love and used only when needed. Its purpose is to guide by encouragement and restraint.

Certainly parental authority can be taken to extremes (and obviously, at times, it is). Too much authority leads to totalitarianism, while too little leads to injustice and social chaos. This is true for nations; it is also true for families.

As we've already mentioned, the middle years are a time of great change not just for your child, but for you as a parent. Perhaps the greatest transition you will experience is that of learning to use less of your authority, and more of your influence, to motivate your child. Here is a basic truism we want you to remember: *When your child was young, you led by the power of your authority. When he or she is a teen, you will lead by the strength of your relational influence. Between the two points the need for parental authority should decline as your child begins to exercise moral self-control.* By the time your child hits adolescence, you will have exchanged rule-centered leadership for principle-centered leadership. Here is an example of what we mean.

At the end of one of our parenting classes, Carla, a young mother of three, approached Anne Marie with a question. She listened attentively to Anne Marie's response, reluctantly agreed to try what she had suggested, and went home. When she returned to class the next week, she enthusiastically shared the following results. Here is a transcript of what she said to an audience of her peers.

> I have three girls. Whitney is ten; Brenda, seven; and Carissa is four. Like most parents, I have a real fear about this next phase of parenting, especially with my ten year old. I had a little talk with Anne Marie last week about an incident involving Whitney and sharing.
>
> I explained to Anne Marie that Whitney had a bag of popcorn and Brenda asked for some. Whitney said no. This really bothered me because my seven year old is so generous with her sister, almost to a fault. So I intervened and told Whitney that she had to share. She finally did.
>
> When I thought through the incident, I knew I hadn't done the right thing, but I didn't know what I had done wrong. So I asked Anne Marie what she thought I should do in such situations. I was surprised

when she told me to think about not always intervening with my authority and forcing my kids to share with each other. This was a frightening prospect for me. I said to Anne Marie, "How long will I be doing this? What if this goes on forever?" Anne Marie assured me it would not, but asked that I try this for several weeks and see what happens.

In God's perfect timing, the next day, another incident took place. Whitney had some mints and Brenda asked for some. Whitney said no, and Brenda immediately looked to me for help. I told Brenda, "If Whitney doesn't want to share with you that's fine. God wants sharing to come from our hearts or it is not real sharing." Brenda protested for a few moments, and I went about my business.

A little later my ten year old came to me and asked: "It's okay if I don't share, Mom? Is that what you said?" I said, "Yes, that's what I said." Whitney left but in that very moment, I could see something had changed in her heart. Five minutes later she was generously sharing all her mints with Brenda.

The next day, all I heard from the two girls was: "Can I borrow your this, can I play with your that?" I was shocked. I thought non-coercive sharing was foreign to my children. It was foreign to me.

So I called my ten year old aside and asked, "Whitney, why are you so willing to share all of a sudden?" And this is what she told me. "Mom, this is how I always felt but you never let me do it without telling me I had to. I wanted to show you how I feel, but you never let me do it without making me. I want to show you that I know how to make a wise decision and do the things you and Daddy taught us."

I went home last week and gave up trying to control all the outcomes by using my authority. In a very marginal way, I started to use the power of my influence by speaking truth in love with my kids. I can tell you, in one week's time, Whitney has become a different child—mostly because she has a different mom. And while I am still using my authority with Brenda, I can see why I need less and less of it to guide Whitney.

There is one more thing I learned through this experience. In the past when I tried to control all outcomes, I was actually robbing my kids of the joy of doing right. I can see that now. At Whitney's age, there is no joy in doing right when the actions required are always tied to my authority.

Can you relate to Carla's story? We sure can. We remember similar situations that occurred during our preteen parenting days. Please note what Carla did *not* do; she did not abandon her God-given authority. What she *did* do was start the process of giving up her power to control all outcomes. Now she works to bring about right outcomes by leading through her influence.

Consider for a moment how you once controlled everything about your child's day. During his infancy, you determined when your child ate, slept, stayed awake, had a bath, played on the blanket, or went for a stroller ride.

Such tight supervision is absolutely necessary during the early years, since a child does not know how to regulate his own day for his own good. But as children grow, they become more responsible. When your child was five, you no longer controlled or directed your child's day to the same extent you did years earlier. At five, children can come and go from the back yard, pick out their own board games, play with their hamsters, or go to their rooms and play with a puzzle. Because they continually demonstrated responsible behavior in these areas, parental policing was no longer necessary. Our point is this: Although parental authority is still a considerable influence in a five-year-old's life, it is not as sweeping in its control as it was a few years earlier.

The same holds true of a ten year old. With the increase of self-rule, there is a direct decrease in the amount of parental policing required. It's not that Mom and Dad's authority is no longer valid, but the need for outside control is diminishing. Gradually, parental control is being replaced by parental influence. External motivations that once governed the child's life are replaced by internal beliefs that rule from the heart. Moral maturity emancipates the child, allowing him to direct his own behavior in harmony with family values.

At this point we want to make clear that we are not suggesting that you eliminate house or family rules. Your middle-years child (and later, your teen) is still accountable to you. There are community tasks and responsibilities that need to be maintained. In other words, your child still needs to take out the trash, make his own bed, clean up after himself, be home at a reasonable hour, and yes, comply with parental instruction. However, the basic tasks of life should take on new meaning—a moral one in response to a relationship to the family. No longer are they simply a response to an impersonal set of rules reinforced by coercive authority.

Like Carla in the example above, you may feel a bit awkward as you begin the exchange of authority for influence. However, this change is absolutely necessary for a successful middle-years transition to occur. Understand, you will use far more of your authority with your eight year old than you will with your twelve year old. But by the end of the middle years, the authority exchange should be complete. Take a moment to consider where you are right now in the process of authority exchange.

MORAL LIVING: MORE THAN WORDS

Just as it is in the body of Christ, whenever there is a breakdown in relationships between family members, the failure ultimately is tied to a breakdown in values. This is why you cannot start to build relational bridges without first having a common source of values. Common values, when Bible-based, are what strengthen family ties. They are the glue that holds families together.

Having common values means that the moral rules children live by are also observed by Mom and Dad. When you remove the possibility of a double standard ("do as I say, not as I do"), you remove the likelihood of hypocrisy. In its place will be relational security, confidence, believability, and trustworthiness.

By the time the middle years are reached, your child should have begun to acquire a moral code to which he or she voluntarily adheres with increasing frequency. The more your preteen voluntarily yields to that code the less parental authority is needed—but equally so, the more parental *example* is required.

A child who has been taught that it is wrong to lie and who attempts to be honest will lose all motivation to live honestly if he sees that his parents do not do so. When a parent violates the truth of a conversation or describes a dubious business deal, he or she loses all credibility in the eyes of the preteen.

Kids are extremely sharp; they notice when there is disparity between our words and actions. Naturally, they conclude: "What's good enough for Mom and Dad is good enough for me." The inconsistency between values preached and values lived will always force a greater need for parental policing than would have been necessary if parents themselves were greater examples of the virtues they tried to instill.

By the time your child reaches moral maturity—between the ages of thirteen and fifteen—your parental authority should be nearly invisible. Though you still exercise it, more often your child's behavior is controlled by voluntary self-rule. Conforming voluntary self-rule means only one thing: relational unity. And a unified family is wonderful.

SUMMARY

During the middle years, children are heading toward adolescence and maturity. During this time, parents lead, guide, and direct their children to virtuous behavior, reinforcing compliance by extrinsic means until the child is morally mature enough to govern himself by intrinsic values. This explanation assumes a decreasing emphasis on leadership by authority and an increasing emphasis on leadership by influence. That is, the more morally mature your child becomes, the less you lead by your authority and the more you lead by your relational influence.

BRINGING IT HOME

1. What is moral maturity and at what age should it show itself?

2. What do permissive and authoritarian parents say about each other?

3. Describe the most important middle-years transition through which parents go.

4. In Carla's story, what was she robbing from Whitney?

5. What role does parental example play in helping a child reach moral maturity?

Chapter Four

How to Raise
a Morally Mature
Middle-Years Child

At a private school with which we are involved, potential students are given a moral readiness evaluation as part of an experiment that measures the relationship between moral excellence and academic mastery.

In one interview, an eight year old was asked, "Elena, if you were sitting on a bus and all the seats were taken, and an older person came on the bus looking for a seat, what would you do?"

Elena put her head down on the desk for a moment, processed the scenario presented, and came up with the following reply.

"It all depends," she said. "If there was a sign on the bus that required children to stay seated while the bus was in motion, then I would scoot over and ask the person to sit next to me. But if there was no sign, I would get up and let the person have my seat. Both ways, I could obey God's request to honor age" (Leviticus 19:32).

Elena's answer is amazing on a number of levels. But what is perhaps most amazing is her introduction of the element: a sign requiring that children remain seated while the bus was in motion. By adding this element, she created a condition in which two competing values of equal weight called for Elena's simultaneous attention: obedience to authority (represented by the sign) and respect for age. In the face of these seemingly conflicting values, her eight-year-old mind processed all the variables and came up with a way to satisfy both values without compromising either.

It is particularly amazing that Elena demonstrated such an ability at the age of eight. Ideally, you want your child to reach moral maturity sometime between the ages of thirteen and fifteen, perhaps even as early as twelve. But how is such moral maturity achieved? And what role do parents play in cultivating or delaying healthy moral attitudes?

This chapter focuses on character development and moral training: how children obtain and internalize their values, and how parents rightly and wrongly pass on these values. Your goal is to help your child achieve, within a few short years, a level of morality that is equal to yours. By the midteen years, you want your child to be your moral peer, to act as a son or daughter of God's moral law.

OUR STORY

We came to understand moral maturity more by accident than design. After receiving several gracious compliments about our own adolescent children, we began to ask ourselves: Why are they this way? What had we done, either purposefully or inadvertently, a few years earlier that helped shape our children's early teen years?

Certainly we enjoyed our children. But equally important was the fact that other people enjoyed them. We wondered: What is it, exactly, that other people enjoy about them? It wasn't their physical maturity; they still had plenty of growing to do. It wasn't their academic or intellectual maturity. They still had plenty of learning ahead of them. Still, there was something about them that put them on an equal footing with adults.

It could be only one thing, we realized—their moral maturity. They had matured in six critical categories of respect. They knew how to relate biblically to authority, their elders, peers, the property of others, and God's world (nature). And they certainly knew how to fulfill the fifth commandment: "Honor your father and your mother" (Exodus 20:12a).

This was true not only of our kids. Think about the young people you know. We have all met teens and preteens who are known for being sociable, courteous, respectful, gracious, motivated, and genuine. There are families all around us with teens of this moral caliber. In these families, love between parent and child is evidenced by their mutual respect for one another and by the absence of rebellious conflict.

How did they get to this point of relational harmony? What is it about these kids that makes being with them enjoyable? What allows you to have fun with them (and them with you) without having to default to a peer status? These kids all share one common trait: a moral maturity that makes being with them an absolute pleasure.

When we say that a child possesses moral maturity, this does not mean he or she is all knowing and all wise in all things. Certainly that is not the case. This does mean, however, that the preteen has come to a place where the values Mom and Dad have been communicating for so many years have at last been internalized.

Children mature physically and intellectually at different rates. Yet it seems that in God's overall design of the four classes of maturity—legal, physical, intellectual, and moral—the one most tied to healthy human relationships is moral maturity. This class is also, when nurtured correctly, the first to blossom.

It should begin to happen soon. Let's look at the steps you'll take in leading your child to moral maturity.

Step One: Teach the way of virtue, not just the avoidance of wrong.

As we studied child-rearing patterns in Christian families over the years, we discovered that parents tend to spend more time and energy suppressing wayward behavior than elevating good behavior in their children. That is, when teaching moral principles, parents will often tell their children what is wrong and what not to do, rather than what is right and what they should do. This type of training leads to serious moral compromise in the future. Because so much emphasis is placed on which behaviors to avoid and too little on which ones to pursue, the path to virtuous deeds is left highly undefined for the child.

Certainly Elena's mom and dad understood the importance of suppressing her self-oriented, wayward behavior. But they also understood that if they suppressed wrong without elevating good, they would ultimately end up distorting the meaning of "good" in Elena's mind. Restraint of wayward behavior must be accompanied by instruction in righteousness and by encouragement in virtuous living (Proverbs 1:1–7; 8:33; 9:9; Micah 6:8).

Eleven-year-old Sandy actively teased her younger sister Cheryl in many unkind ways. Friends would hear Sandy's secrets, but Sandy publicly excluded Cheryl from sharing in this knowledge. When the two girls rode bikes together, Sandy predictably caused Cheryl to fall off and get hurt. Sandy would also manipulate situations to gain an advantage over her sister, often at the expense of her sister's feelings. The girls' mom corrected each occurrence by punishing Sandy, but could not understand why such exaggerated one-sided sibling conflict continued.

This mother failed to realize the principle above. Yes, she temporarily suppressed Sandy's wayward behavior by correcting each occurrence, but that's what led to the perpetual problem. She focused so much on unkind behavior that she failed to routinely teach the necessity of being kind. She was reactive when it came to wrong, but not proactive when it came to teaching that which is right and virtuous.

Restraining wrong has to be balanced by elevating good. Moral restraint and moral assertiveness are two sides of the same coin. Both must be taught by parents if a child is to have a healthy perspective of right and wrong, good and evil.

Step Two: Know that moral training begins in parents' hearts.

Moral training begins with Mom and Mad. In Deuteronomy 6:4–6, Moses gave instructions on how the Israelites were to live in their new land. Speaking of God's moral requirements, he said, "Hear O Israel: The LORD our God, the LORD is one! You shall love the LORD your God with all your heart, with all your soul, and with all your might. And these words, which I command you today shall be in your heart."

Effective parents know they cannot lead their child any further than they have gone themselves. They realize that God's moral law, the prescription for moral living that reflects the will and character of God, must be in their own hearts before it can be passed on to their children.

Here we offer this timeless warning: Just because a parent has advanced moral knowledge does not mean he or she is a moral person. A moral lifestyle does not automatically follow moral knowledge.

As parents, we must live our Christianity, not just talk about it. One of the great credibility builders of parenthood is personal integrity. On the other hand, one of the most destructive forces in parenting is hypocrisy. Parental hypocrisy occurs when Mom and Dad exempt themselves from the set of values they require their children to uphold. Hypocrisy breeds contempt, leading to future relational breakdown.

That is why the moral rules we require our children to follow must also apply to us. There can be no double standard in the Christian home. A Father cannot lecture on honesty and then, when the phone rings, say to his wife, "Tell them I'm not home." As parents we must live our Christianity, not just preach it.

We must also continually grow in the knowledge of God's moral law. Applying God's moral law to our own lives legitimizes the instruction we give our kids. This is important because during the middle years, more than ever before, our kids are watching every move we make.

Step Three: Know the how and why of moral training.

Many children know how to apply moral law, but not as many know the "why" behind it. Knowing how to do right and why it is so, are distinctly two different things. The first represents an action; the second represents the principle behind the action. Often children are taught what they should not do (e.g., do not steal) or should do (e.g., share your toys with your sister). However, parents in our society consistently fail to teach the moral or practical reason of the behavior. This results in children who are outwardly, but not inwardly, moral. They know how to respond in different circumstances only because they have been trained to the circumstance, not because they understand the moral principle involved.

Like Elena, eight-year-old Robby went through the Community School's interview process to determine his moral readiness. One of the scenarios presented to him was: "Robby, imagine that you and your family are eating dinner at Mr. and Mrs. Brown's house. After dinner, Mrs. Brown brings out a beautiful cake and starts to pass out pieces to everyone including herself. She then takes the cake and returns it to the kitchen. When would you start eating your piece of cake?"

Robby answered, "After Mrs. Brown sat down and started to eat her dessert." His answer speaks to the moral behavior insisted upon by his parents. Next he was asked a more specific question: "Robby, tell us why you would wait?" Because his parents had taught him the moral "why" of the behavior, Robby knew the reason for his action. He responded with a very simple explanation: "Because love is not rude" (1 Corinthians 13:5a). "It would be rude not to wait for the one who served us." Here is an example of a child who is in the process of becoming morally aware. Not only does he know *what* to do, he understands the "why" behind it.

It is not enough to teach your children how to act morally; they must learn to think morally as well. Children who do all the right things without knowing why these things are right are moral robots. They often respond to situations and circumstances correctly, but not from any guiding principles of the heart. In contrast, children who govern their behavior by moral principle are anything but robots. They are morally free, governing their behavior by intrinsic principle, not extrinsic circumstances.

Does this step obligate you to provide a "why" explanation upon your child's demand? Of course not. There will be plenty of times during the middle years when the explanation is simply "because Mom (or Dad) said so." But by the time your child hits the middle years, instructions that are tied to morality should include moral or practical reasons why. Without principles stirring the heart, a child is limited in just how inwardly motivated he or she will become.

Step Four: Provide the practical "why."

Not every explanation offered by parents will be associated with moral training. Some explanations serve only a practical purpose. As a general rule, parents should offer a moral reason in a situation which concerns people and a practical reason in a situation relating to things.

For example, Shayla's dad was working on a weed problem near the fruit tree. His busyness attracted her curiosity. Seeing his daughter draw near, he warned, "Shayla, move away from the tree. I just sprayed poison around the trunk, and it's not safe." In this situation, there was a practical reason (health and safety) why Shayla's behavior needed to be restrained, not a moral one. Since Shayla received practical information about what was going on by the tree, her curiosity was not further challenged. That information minimized the tension between Shayla's need for obedience and her natural curiosity. Her dad satisfied her childlike need to investigate.

Step Five: Make moral judgments by examining context.

How can you know if what you are allowing your child to do offends or advances biblical truth? Consider this true-to-life example. After morning services, little Stevie Brown was running recklessly on the church patio. Stevie's dad, observing the crowd, suggested to his wife that Stevie should stop. But Stevie's mom said, "He's not hurting anything. Let him run." Is there a moral issue in this scenario that should be acted upon? Is there something biblically wrong with running?

We cannot classify an action as acceptable or unacceptable without first placing it in its context. The consideration of context is critically important in the parenting process. The context of any given situation allows a parent to focus on the right response without compromising moral truth. Context is what helps determine whether an action complements or detracts from biblical principles.

In the case of Stevie, the action of a little boy running may appear to be morally neutral. Certainly, no Bible verses prohibit such innocent play. But, when you put his running into context—a patio filled with elderly people, younger children, those in wheelchairs, and mothers with babies—little Stevie's behavior is no longer morally neutral but morally unacceptable. Although there is no verse that speaks directly to his action, the principles of consideration, esteeming others more highly than ourselves, and respect for age all do speak to it. Stevie's behavior demonstrates a lack of concern and respect for the welfare of others. It is his parents' responsibility to stop him from running and to explain the problem to him.

In contrast to Stevie's actions, young Donna stood close to her parents' side. Although she wanted to join Stevie's play, they said she could not. Donna's parents then did what is truly reflective of biblical training: they explained why running was not appropriate on the church patio. They considered the welfare and feelings of others and made a judgment as to what would be the most appropriate behavior under the circumstances. Then they explained their decision.

They helped Donna see the potential dangers and taught her why standing by their side was the best thing to do given the present circumstances. Rather than issuing the sweeping command, "Don't run" (a general rule that would not be applicable under all circumstances), they trained their daughter in the biblical principle that governed the moment. By training her to principle, they trained her to be morally discerning. When a similar situation presents itself in the future, Donna will be prepared to respond according to principle. This time her behavior was governed by Mom and Dad; next time she will be able to govern her own behavior based on what she learned to be right.

What would have happened if Donna's parents had not given her the reason for their restriction? What we consistently find is this: today's "no" is only for today and not because of the violation of any principle. The next time a similar situation presents itself, Donna would have no basis upon which to decide. She simply would not have any moral reasons not to run. The absence of moral reason often gets children into trouble.

Step Six: Avoid legalism when giving instruction.

In an attempt to ensure moral compliance, some parents go to the dangerous extreme of labeling every behavior either right or wrong, without any consideration given to the circumstance. But making such sweeping statements is neither accurate nor appropriate. This is when legalism takes over. Legalism creates prohibitions by elevating a method over biblical principle. When we value the law more than we do grace, or when we regard man-made traditions as highly as we do God's Word (as did the Pharisees), we succumb to legalism. Legalists tend to see all decisions in life as either right (moral) or wrong (immoral).

We have all heard the exhortation "Let's keep things in context." The most notable aspect of a legalist is this: he rejects context. Responding to the context of a situation does not mean that we should suspend biblical laws or principles. It means that we should apply them in the most appropriate way. Considering context guards us against legalism.

Let's go back to Donna and her parents. What if they had said, "Donna, while at church you are *never* to run on this patio"? Do her parents really mean never? What if she was called upon to get the church nurse or doctor for an emergency? Could she run under those circumstances? What if there was a fire? Could she run then? Donna's parents understand that their child is better served by knowing the principles behind the law, than simply the letter of the law.

SUMMARY

The Bible represents ultimate authority and moral sufficiency. In its pages are the moral virtues that reflect God's righteousness and wisdom. There are no moral variations in its precepts. The values that govern conduct and define good and evil are the same for all people and for all time.

Christian parents need to realize that it is not enough to teach their children how to act morally; they must also teach them how to think morally. To accomplish that goal, parents themselves must think in accordance with biblical values. That thinking is the prerequisite to the process of raising a morally responsible child.

The lack of biblical values in our society threatens each subsequent generation. As each generation becomes more desensitized to the precious nature of others, we will inevitably move to the generation that will mark the point of no return. As it has been said: What one generation will allow in moderation, the next will allow in excess.

BRINGING IT HOME

1. When teaching moral principles, often parents will tell their children what is wrong and what not to do, rather than what is right and what they should do. What is wrong with this practice?

2. What is one of the most destructive forces in parenting, as described in Step Two? Explain.

3. What is the difference between knowing *how* to do right and *why* it is so?

4. In our story above, what mistakes did Sandy's mother make as she tried to suppress her daughter's wayward behavior?

5. Why is context so important in the parenting process?

Chapter Five

BEYOND BASIC PARENTING: RAISING THE STANDARD

Not too many years ago, we went to Arizona to visit some church representatives working in our ministry. When we got out of the car, we noticed eight-year-old Timarie standing on the sidewalk waiting for our arrival and subsequent visit with her parents. We made eye contact and said, "Hello. Are you one of the Lambrose children?"

"Yes," she responded. Then she walked toward us with adult-like confidence and put out her hand to shake ours. As she graciously looked into our eyes, she said with all sincerity, "Hello, Mr. and Mrs. Ezzo. It is very nice to meet you. Did you have a nice trip over to Tucson?"

Were we impressed? Yes, very much so. Timarie's interest in us was clearly genuine. A few minutes later, we met her siblings who, in their own way, demonstrated the same moral sensitivity. Later in our visit we asked the parents what they did to bring their children to this level of moral sincerity. They told us they had taught their children three levels of moral responses: *good, better* and *best.*

Doing *good,* they explained to their kids, represents who you are as a person. It also represents the minimum courtesy required in a moral situation. If someone said "hello," Timarie and her siblings knew that the appropriate response was to acknowledge the greeter by saying "hello" in return. If the person extended a compliment, such as, "Those are pretty ribbons in your hair, Timarie," the minimum courtesy would be to say, "Thank-you."

Doing *better*, the parents went on to say, represents our family: who we are and what we stand for. *Better* takes us beyond the moral minimum to the next step in extending a courtesy. For example, Timarie's parents encouraged and showed their children how to reach out and shake hands with any adult to whom they were introduced. They stressed that greeting a person with the eyes is just as important as shaking hands. They also taught that if a child or adult is sitting when a visitor walks into the room, that person is to stand and acknowledge the newcomer's presence. Such a gesture is based on 1 Corinthians 13:5: love is not rude.

Doing what is *best*, this couple taught their kids, represents God. This involves going over and above what is required. Rather than simply saying "hi" in response to the extension of a hand, the children become the initiators of kindness. Not only did Timarie say "hello" and walk toward us with her hand extended, she also initiated conversation: "Did you have a nice trip over to Tucson?" Those few words went a long way. *Good* is acceptable and *better* is preferable. But *best,* seeking to please God, is most desirable.

When young Timarie extended her hand and asked about our welfare, she was extending a courtesy the best way she knew how. This wasn't anything her parents required of her. It wasn't an obedience issue. It was part of the training and the teaching process in which she had been involved throughout her childhood.

Proverbs 20:11 tells us, "Even a child is known by his deeds, by whether what he does is pure and right." A child's moral disposition will show itself. Just as the new bud leads to a blossom and the blossom to fruit, what is in your child's heart will blossom some day.

The apostle Paul told the Philippian church to "approve the things that are excellent" (Philippians 1:10a). The word *approve* means, literally, to test the way of excellence; to know what is genuine. The word for excellence, the Greek *diaphero* means to do over and above; and to go beyond what is required. This does not mean that we are striving for perfection; perfectionists do not enjoy the real world because they are critical of themselves and often critical of the shortcomings of others. However, we should be striving for moral excellence, not mediocrity, when it comes to "do all to the glory of God" (1 Corinthians 10:31).

How can you teach your middle-years child to approve that which is excellent? How do you get your preteen to "go beyond what is required" with the values that are in his or her heart? How can you move your son or daughter beyond just the external compliance to the letter of the law? There must come a time when your child goes beyond the minimum requirement and pursues the way of excellence.

Timarie's moral disposition showed itself through right principles—because right principles were placed there by her parents. It is now time to take your middle-years child to the next level of moral sensitivity. Go beyond *good* and *better*. Encourage your preadolescent to strive for *best*—the excellencies found in Christ.

SELF-GENERATED MORALITY

Children make moral decisions every day. Some of their decisions are prohibitive in nature, meaning that children make them in order to avoid wrong. By not doing wrong, the children are in effect doing something right. By not throwing trash on the sidewalk, he is acting virtuously. By not returning evil for evil, he is exalting virtue. This is *prohibitive morality.*

Other decisions are made in response to a moral prompting.

Such *prompted morality* takes place when the child responds to moral cues, such as saying "thank you" when a compliment is extended. In this case the moral response offered by the child was prompted by someone or something outside the child.

There is also a third level of morality: one that Timarie and her siblings had already reached, one that our kids reached, and one that your kids certainly can reach. This level is called *self-generated morality* and it comes from within.

How is your child progressing in the three levels of morality described above?

SELF-GENERATED INITIATIVE

Not long ago, a couple named Barb and Phil came to us with questions about their five children (ranging from seven to fourteen in age). Barb and Phil felt that something was wrong with their children's moral development but didn't know what it was. Their kids demonstrated kindness, great table manners, and self-control; responded politely when spoken to; and were courteous to strangers. Basically, they were all-around great kids. Yet, there was a gap in their character. There was something missing in their moral profile that their parents—and we—could not identify right away.

Over the next several months we had the opportunity to observe the children in a number of different settings. But it was not until one of our own adult children spent time with the family one weekend that the discovery was made. Our daughter Jennifer picked up on a factor many parents miss—all five of these kids lacked *self-generated initiative.*

Self-generated initiative is the highest and most desirable level of moral motivation. At this level, a child responds to needs without prompting or instruction. In Sunday school, Barb and Phil's children would never knowingly drop a piece of paper on the floor and walk away from it. And, if their teacher asked them to pick up a piece of paper lying on the floor, they would happily do so. But if the teacher did not instruct them to pick up the piece of paper, they would not have done it on their own.

This was what was missing in the children's moral profile. While they would do all things heartily unto the Lord when prompted, they lacked initiative to do right without prompting.

The most exciting and encouraging aspect of this story is how quickly the problem was fixed. Barb and Phil realized what they needed to do: teach their kids about self-generated initiative, both by conversation and by action. They posted three-by-five cards all around the house, upon which these words were written: "Don't wait to be asked to do good, before doing good." In less than two weeks that slogan paid big dividends. Self-generated initiative had become a part of their children's character.

A CASE FOR EMPATHY

During your child's early years you began to work on a crucial aspect of his or her moral development: learning godly values. This was important because when there are no heavenly values to stir the heart, the heart will not be stirred toward righteousness. Most children know how to apply moral law. They have been taught what to do and what not to do. But few know the moral reason why. This is tragic, because without the why, there can be no empathy.

At creation, God instilled in man a wide range of emotions: anger, joy, disappointment, guilt, sadness, peace, contentment, and fear, to name a few. Out of this list, certain emotions are triggered by encounters with morality. Shame, guilt, and empathy are three of them.

Empathy is the ability to enter into another's emotions and, when appropriate, to act on those feelings. Sooner or later empathy becomes the barometer of moral maturity. Children who know the how but not the why of moral law also lack the ability to express empathy. If your child is trained to the letter of the law and not to the principle that the law represents, then his or her ability to empathize is hindered.

Falling out of Bed

The following example illustrates this point. When Jerry's dad said, "Stay in bed, Son, and leave the light off," he was expecting total compliance. However, when Jerry's little brother, Sammy, fell out of bed in the middle of the night, Jerry got up and turned on a light in order to help him. Jerry understood his father's instruction. He also understood the context and purpose for which they were given. He knew it was not his father's intent to keep him in bed under any circumstances.

He could have obeyed the letter of the law and stayed in bed. But to do so would have compromised the greater need of the moment—comforting his younger brother and helping him back into bed. Not only would the greater good have been compromised, his failure to provide comfort to a frightened sibling would have created a greater wrong. Given these options, Jerry chose to respond with empathy.

He was able to regulate his behavior because he was trained to the biblical principle, not simply to the letter of the law. More than that, he possessed a healthy degree of self-generated initiative. He did not wait until he heard from the other room, "Jerry, help your brother." Rather, he acted on his moral knowledge and did that which he knew to be right.

Your middle-years child, too, must step beyond external obedience. To help your child achieve this level of sensitivity, you must move him or her 1) from outward compliance to the letter of the law, 2) to inward understanding of the principle behind the law, and 3) to a place where he or she can begin taking action based on empathy.

As Easy as... Cake

Let's look at another snapshot of this. Dave and Kim were looking forward to a visit from their old friends Larry and Sue, whom they had not seen since their ministry years back in Nebraska. For dessert that night, Kim baked Larry's favorite cake, topping it with a special maple frosting. After she was finished, Kim placed it on the kitchen table. She turned to ten-year-old Nate, who was sitting at the counter working on a puzzle, and said, "Now, Nate, don't take a swipe of frosting with your finger. In fact, I don't want you to touch the cake at all. It's a surprise dessert for Mr. Miller. I'm going next door, but I'll be back in half an hour."

Kim left the kitchen, and Nate continued working his puzzle. But a few minutes later he noticed that the angle of the sun was changing. Hot rays began to stream in through the window, falling on the cake. He soon realized that if the cake was not moved, the frosting would melt and the dessert would be ruined.

At this point, Nate was confronted with a moral decision. The letter of the law said, "Don't touch the cake at all." But the intent of the law was also made known: "It's a surprise dessert for Mr. Miller." The intent was communicated as part of the instructions, and that is how Nate decided what to do. He considered his mother's order, but he also considered what she really meant by it. She meant that he was not to consume any part of the cake. She wanted the cake to remain intact so it could be a gift to the Millers. Understanding the principle behind the law gave Nate the freedom to do that which was right. It allowed him to act with empathy, without fear.

Nate understood his mom's desire to do something special for the Millers. He knew how disappointed she would be if the cake was ruined because of a simple oversight and his lack of action. The principle of empathy was at work in Nate's heart. He was trained to look beyond the law to the greater principle. He took ownership of his mom's feelings and acted on them by moving the cake out of the sun's rays.

He could have done nothing and still have met the letter of the law. But like Jerry in our previous illustration, he did that which was best, or morally superior. He considered his mother, her feelings, and the circumstances, then acted on them empathetically.

THE EARLY SIGNS OF MORAL MATURITY

Another example of empathetic behavior involves ten-year-old Ryan, who was supervising his younger brothers and their school friends in an informal soccer game while their parents attended a teacher's meeting. Jill and her parents had come directly from a wedding, so Jill had no play clothes. She stood on the side line with her white dress and shiny black shoes and watched the other kids play. Ryan, realizing that his classmate could not join in because of her clothing, called the other kids over and started playing something that Jill could participate in. Ryan considered Jill, her feelings of non-involvement, the circumstances that prevented her participation, and acted out of empathy. Does your child have the moral knowledge and convictions to do the same?

SUMMARY

Your middle-years child should now be in the process of acquiring a set of personal values to which he or she adheres with increasing frequency. In the Christian home, this moral adherence is driven by three factors: moral knowledge (What does God's moral law say?), moral reason (What does the law mean?), and last but certainly not least, parental example (How valid is the law in the life of those insisting on it?).

If moral knowledge, moral reason, and parental example are lived out in your home today, you will have an extraordinarily wonderful relationship when your son or daughter reaches the teen years. This is because values of the heart are the greatest influence on relationships. Common values unify, while conflicting values war against intimate healthy relationships. This is especially true during your child's upcoming teen years. Take a moment to consider what is in your child's heart today. Who has shaped his or her morality?

BRINGING IT HOME

1. Explain the three moral responses of *good, better,* and *best.*

2. What is the difference between prompted morality and self-generated moral initiative?

3. What is empathy?

4. Would empathy be more closely associated with prompted initiative or moral initiative?

5. Moral adherence is driven by what three factors? Explain how this occurs.

Chapter Six

THE POWER
OF GROUPTHINK

As she walked by her preteen's open bedroom door, Angela noticed eleven-year-old Jillian staring intently into her closet. At the sight of her daughter's furrowed brow, Angela stopped at the doorway and asked, "Is everything ok, honey?"

"Fine, Mom." Jillian continued to gaze in the direction of her closet.

Angela walked into Jillian's room. Once inside, she saw what had captured her daughter's attention: two very stylish, very different dresses hanging from the closet door.

She smiled knowingly. "Trying to decide which one you want to wear to the school awards banquet?"

"Uh-huh." Jillian nodded seriously.

"Well, I think the blue one looks the nicest on you," Angela told her daughter helpfully.

"Really?" Angela looked sideways at her mom. She appeared doubtful.

"Oh, yes. It's always been my favorite."

"Wel-l-l..." Jillian hesitated, then seemed to make a decision. She turned and stepped toward the door—and the direction of the hall phone. "I think I'd better call Erin and see what she thinks."

Angela and Jillian's story is not uncommon. Perhaps you've experienced a similar scene in your own home. Whereas Jillian once valued her mother's opinion above all others, suddenly her friends' opinions—what we refer to as "groupthink"—carries more weight than ever before.

Although socializing with children of the same age is a natural part of growing up, it's not until the middle and early teen years that a child becomes fully aware of what it means to belong to a group of peers. And it is not until this time that parents really begin to understand the full impact of peer relationships.

You've probably noticed by now that your family is not the only influence on your child. During the middle years, peer culture is a growing influence on how he or she thinks and acts. Teachers, coaches, Sunday school workers, and other family members all continue to make an impact. But none of them shape behavior as easily—or in quite the same way—as the combination of hormones and an age-related peer.

HORMONES, BODY CHANGES, AND PEERS

There are very definite connections between hormones, body changes, and social peer pressure. Here are three examples.

A Growing Interest in the Opposite Sex

Many parents of preteens don't want to hear that their children are starting to feel drawn to the opposite sex. However, this is a reality for middle-years children.

It begins at the onset of puberty when boys and girls begin to change their minds about the opposite sex. Not long ago, the girls thought the boys were "icky." But suddenly, boys are starting to look good to the girls, and vice versa. There is a natural attraction. By "attraction," we are not implying any type of sexual fantasy. We simply mean that members of the opposite sex are starting to be more appealing. The girls are looking at the boys and the boys are looking at the girls. Interestingly, they are also noticing that other girls are looking at boys and that some of the boys are looking at the girls. A new awareness of the opposite sex is taking place. This is a part of the hormonal nudge.

A Greater Sensitivity to Differences Between Self and Peers

During the middle years, both boys and girls begin to notice that the peer group is changing. For the most part, girls change sooner than boys, and they start to compare the changes that are taking place.

This can cause preteens to get very emotional at times. When this happens, it is important for us as parents to come alongside and help them see what Mom and Dad's physical structures are like.

Perhaps you have a son who has recently returned to school after summer vacation. He sees that many of his peers have shot up five or six inches, while he remains the same height. He is now looking around, thinking, "What's wrong with me?"

Dad, it's your responsibility—and privilege—to come alongside your son and talk through both the situation and his feelings. It may be appropriate to say, "Well, you take after me, Son," or to simply let him know that in time, he will grow.

Boys also can be clumsy at this age. Often bodies don't grow proportionally. Perhaps his body grows and his head stays small, or his head grows while his body lags behind. Meanwhile the girls are getting prettier. Your son may feel insecure about how they will perceive him. There is a whole new awareness of his physical being.

This is not a sinful awareness of self. Your child is simply noticing, "I'm growing up; he's growing up. But he seems to be growing up faster than I."

Mom and Dad, your preteen will need your support as he or she begins to work through these natural comparisons.

An Indirect Effect on the Parent/Child Relationship

As your middle-years child grows and develops hormones, he or she will begin to look at both the opposite sex and at him- or herself. Not only is there a new awareness and sensitivity in regard to the group, but also a greater need to be doing what the others are doing. Thus the "group" begins to mean more to your child.

Let's say you and your family live in Kristin Howard's neighborhood. Recently you've noticed that little Kristen is developing into a lovely young lady. You realize that your son has noticed this as well, so you're not surprised when he tells you that instead of doing his homework he wants to go riding with "the kids" in the neighborhood. He's not going to come right out and say, "I want to go to Kristen's house." But he will resist doing his homework if it interferes with seeing her.

As long as you ignore the heart of the issue, you and your son will have conflict about the homework. The healthiest thing you can do is deal with it head-on. Sit down with your son and say, "Now, what really is the issue?" Start opening up the lines of communication so you can enter into a deep and meaningful conversation.

The bottom line is this: Hormones may affect the body, but hormones do not affect the heart. The values that you place in the heart, and not the hormones, will drive the child. Make sure those values are there. Make sure that you're working on Philippians 1:10, approving that which is excellent. Make sure you're teaching your child about good, better, and best. All these things we've talked about will ultimately bring harmony to your family and bring your child to moral maturity.

WHAT DOES THE GROUP THINK?

As we discussed above, your middle-years child is now moving from a gentle awakening to a full awareness of the significance of his or her group's opinion. Much of this change is hormone-activated. This is what brings about age-related peer relationships and thus peer pressure. Not only does the child want to know "What does the group think?" more importantly he or she wants to know "What does the group think of me?"

It is a natural human tendency to seek social approval. Think back to when you were a preteen. Remember how much you wanted to be a part of the group, and how wonderful it felt when they included you? Today, you probably feel many of those same feelings about your adult peer groups. You want to be accepted. Your child feels the same.

These feelings are normal, but also can be dangerous. A child's sense of social belonging often is tied to how well he or she meets peer group standards and expectations. As a result of this, preteens quickly learn that if they deviate even slightly from the group's standards, they may be ridiculed or even rejected. Thus, peer pressure brings about the need to conform.

To most of us, the words "peer pressure" have a negative connotation. Yet in and of itself, peer pressure is not evil. It is simply a socializing force that challenges the status quo of a person's thinking and behavior. Peer pressure on middle-years children is not always negative. In fact, it becomes so only when the peer culture's values oppose those of the parents.

To ensure peer acceptance under such conditions, the middle-years child learns that he must accept the group's interests and values. He cannot afford to be different because this would jeopardize his status within the group. To demonstrate his allegiance, he acts out his new association and conforms to the group's identity. This might be represented by choices in hairstyle, clothes, music, and the use of slang or foul language. The child must assess and decide what is more significant: the approval of his peers or the approval of his parents—or find for himself a happy medium.

A GROWING INTEREST IN THE GROUP

Think back to the days when your child was between the ages of two and four. You may recall that at that time, he or she didn't really care about the group. The only time small children will stay with the group is when older kids within it show attention to them. If the older kids stop playing with the younger ones, they will go off to the toy room and find something else to do. The group is just not interesting enough, on its own, to keep their attention.

Between the ages of four and eight, however, children become more interested in the group. It now has momentary significance to them. These kids may play football, even if they don't like the game, simply because they like the group. There's a growing interest in the power of being associated with a group, though often that interest is only temporary.

Between the ages of eight and nineteen, the group starts taking on an even greater significance for the preadolescent and the adolescent. The group's opinion now means more than ever. If all of the nine-year-old girls in your daughter's class are wearing green and your daughter is not, that's going to mean something to her. If she is a Brownie or a Bluebird and all the other girls are wearing a uniform, it will be vital to her that she wear one as well. If all the other boys are wearing their baseball hats to school, your son probably will too. Right now wearing green, or wearing a cap to school, is pretty benign. No one is being hurt by such actions, and no values are being compromised. But morally neutral peer pressure can quickly turn ugly and bring morally challenging peer pressure.

In the years ahead, your child is going to be pulled in many different moral directions. The world is filled with a wide variety of value systems, and for the first time he or she will be faced with these alternative values. During this time you must protect your child from negative peer pressure while reinforcing your family values.

COMBATING NEGATIVE PEER PRESSURE

It's interesting to note that it is a conflict in values, and not the power of peer pressure itself, that tears adolescents from their parents. The closer the values between parents and child, the stronger the family allegiance will be. This significantly decreases the likelihood that a child will drift away from Mom and Dad during the teen years.

Please understand that the healthy family does not eliminate normal peer pressure as much as it develops healthy ways to deal with it. This is why it is wrong to blame peer pressure as the primary cause of drug use, crime, rebellion, sexual promiscuity, and the general breakdown of the family. Fundamentally, the problem is a matter of incompatible values.

Thankfully, there are things you can do to protect your children from negative peer pressure while reinforcing your values. In order for this to happen, you must take advantage of three important resources: 1) the power of family identity, 2) the power of community, and 3) the power of sanctifying grace.

THE POWER OF FAMILY IDENTITY

One of your most effective tools in fighting peer pressure is family identity. What, exactly, is this resource? Put simply, it is your family members' mutual acceptance of who you are as a group and the values to which you ascribe. Identity association is a dynamic found in all human relationships. It is a socializing process by which a person identifies himself with a group he is familiar with, attracted to, or feels empathy with. We derive from our identity associations our sense of belonging, and we give back to these associations varying degrees of allegiance.

Among behavioral scientists, it is commonly accepted that preteens and teens are driven by a natural quest to find their own identity, and that they use peers to help establish and then validate what they believe. However, that's not true of children who are members of an interdependent family: that is, a family in which members are mutually dependent. Within the comfortable confines of the interdependent family, parents, not peers, usually have the greater influence on the preteen.

The very nature of progressive development requires that preteens and teens choose their community identity (that is, their peer friends) only after their family identity is first established, then accepted or rejected. If the family is accepted as the primary source of values and comfort, then the child not only identifies with home, but makes friends from among those possessing similar values. This creates positive peer pressure. When there is harmony between the core beliefs of parents and child, both seek similar values in other families and friends. That is why, ultimately, the peer pressure felt by a child is only as strong as his or her family identity is weak.

Values-based parenting wonderfully facilitates the natural process by which children first associate with their parents, then gain a sense of belonging, and finally pledge their allegiance to the family. In healthy families, adolescence is not a time when teens seek a new identity. Rather, it is a time when they attempt to validate the identity they already have. Any identity crisis for these kids took place at age two, not at fifteen.

Unless driven away by unmet relational needs, preteens and teens don't seek a primary identity apart from their families. Despite what some would have us believe, there is no hidden, genetically controlled, instinctive dynamic whereby kids automatically reject their parents and family in favor of peers—and that's good news for family relationships.

Building Family Identity Takes Time

Today, life seems to be speeding by faster than ever before. At times, it seems that the pace of everything has been accelerated, including the rate at which our children grow. Within a few years, your preadolescent will be on the brink of adulthood. When that happens, will "time" be on your side? When your child is ready to leave the nest, will he or she have fond memories of family interactions—memories that anchor that child back to you?

Think back to the characteristics common to healthy families found in chapter 1. Characteristic number five states that, "Healthy families make time to be with each other and to attend each others events." Such families know they must schedule times to be together or "the tyranny of the urgent" will drive them apart. Family nights, family outings, family vacations—these all give children memories that last a lifetime. This is important not just here and now but, perhaps more critically, for tomorrow. Healthy family times produce a sense of tradition that gives our children and us a sense of belonging.

Traditions tie together our immediate family, as well as each subsequent generation. Every year we sit around the Thanksgiving Day dinner table with our children and our grandchildren. Sooner or later the conversation always seems to come around to "Hey, Dad, do you remember when we used to...?" or "Mom, do you remember that time when we came in from the pouring rain and you...?" Light hearted laughter follows. Our grandchildren watch us share joyful family memories. What does it make them want to do? Be a part of the joy.

Building family identity through the middle years requires that family members schedule time together. You must put family events and times on the calendar and participate in them religiously. A healthy sense of family traditions, a wonderful thing to give to grandchildren, starts with the family times you experience today.

THE POWER OF COMMUNITY

As family educators and as parents, we believe strongly in family identity. But even family identity is not sufficient to carry you through the preteen years. You need something more, something bigger than your family. You need the power of community.

The word "community" can mean many things. We use it to refer to a society of families, tied together, sharing common interests, values, and a significant commitment to an ideal, for the mutual benefit of the individual and the collective membership. In other words, to quote the Three Musketeers: "All for one and one for all!"

Why is it important to have a community? Because a community does something that nothing else can: it establishes within the group a sense of "we-ness" that encourages members to work toward a common good.

Connecting with a Moral Community

Since members of your community are going to teach your children (directly or indirectly), it is vital that you surround yourself with people who share your morals and values. In a moral community you will find people who, like you, are striving to live out the biblical precepts of respect and honor, and to instill in their children a biblical awareness and consideration of others. These are the kind of people who can also provide a support group for you, Mom and Dad.

Another reason you need a like-minded moral community is that it is within your community—whatever that community may be—that your child will find other kids with whom they'll spend their time. You want them to be healthy, moral kids—kids whose moms and dads are working to instill biblical values in their hearts, just as you are with your child.

In the years ahead, broader interests and attachment to friends will become more meaningful to your son or daughter. In the truest sense, he or she is becoming morally and relationally emancipated and self-reliant. That is why the moral community in which you and your child belong will either be a friend or foe to your family values.

Remember, the greater the disparity between the values of your family and your family community (from which you and your child will both draw your peers), the greater will be the source of conflict within the home. The opposite of this is also true: Shared values between community and home result in positive peer pressure on your child.

Being immersed in a moral community is absolutely necessary if you hope to have your values reinforced. When your child's peers come out of a like-minded community, he or she will be reassured of the importance of family values. Furthermore, confidence in you, Mom and Dad, is strengthened. Once your child finds friends in your moral community, those friends become a source of positive peer pressure and healthy groupthink.

This truth is illustrated by the story of a young girl we

know whose orthodontist decided that she needed to wear headgear. Though he strongly recommended that she wear the headgear twenty-four hours a day, he said to her with the greatest sensitivity, "I realize, though, that you probably can't wear it at school because the kids might laugh at you."

"Oh, no," the girl told him. "Not at my school. The kids won't laugh at me there." This child felt secure in her community. She knew she would not be ridiculed. This gave her the strength she needed to help her do what she knew was best: wear the headgear at all times.

How would your child respond in this situation? Would the children in his or her circle of friends say, "Do what's right. Wear the headgear"? Or would they say, "Don't listen to your mom and dad. You look like a dork"?

At this point, we must make one important clarification: By stating that you must surround your family with people who share your morals and values, we are not saying that you should isolate your children from the world. Nothing could be further from the truth. To isolate yourself into a moral community is as unbiblical as it is to say that you don't need a moral community to help you raise your children.

Parents should not isolate children from nonbelievers. Jesus calls us to be salt and light to the world (Matthew 5:13–14). However, we do want to insulate our children from corruptive influences.

When our family lived in New England years ago, every floor, ceiling, and outside wall was insulated. As parents, we insulated our home because we did not want the elements to disturb the healthy environment we were providing for our children. That insulation did not keep every element out. Yes, it slowed the process of cold coming into our house. But it did not keep the wind from rushing in when the door was opened. It was also true that we could not stay in the house all the time. It was necessary and important for us to go out into the world around us. The insulated house did, however, give us a place where we could find safety and warmth.

By the same token, a moral community insulates your child against the elements of the world. Through association with like-minded peers, our children see family standards reinforced by others who share the same values. The strength they draw from moral peers is the very thing that makes it possible for Mom and Dad to let them participate in city Little League or a community soccer league. The support of moral community allows our families to go and minister, knowing that the moral strength drawn from our like-minded community allows us to present something very beautiful to the world.

THE CITY GATE

Having a moral community is important. But now we're going to take this idea one step further and tell you that not only do you need a community that includes peers, you need a community that includes elders. Think for a moment about the people who are in your family's community. Within that mix, who are the parents who have gone before you? Who are the ones leading you? Where do you get your wisdom? It all boils down to the question: Who are the elders in your community?

Psalms 127 gives a beautiful biblical analogy of the elders sitting at the gate. In this passage, the elders are the ones to whom people go for wisdom; the gate is the place where the elders can be found. When men and women of the Old Testament needed counsel on the sale of property, help with a business investment, or wisdom on how to deal with a troublesome child, they knew where to go. They went to the city gate, the place of the elders. Today, we still need counsel in all these areas. Yet, sadly, we have lost our respect for the "aged ones" who carry wisdom in their bosom. Think about it. Who are the elders at your gate?

Not only is it good for you, Mom and Dad, to have this resource, it is also comforting for your child to know that their parents have someone older and wiser to whom they can go for advice. As you seek wisdom from elders, you are setting a silent example. Your child sees that you know you need wisdom from an elder who knows what you are going through. As a result, he or she will be more inclined to come to you for wisdom, or even one of your peers, than to his or her peers when the need for guidance arises.

FINDING YOUR ELDERS

As you consider the questions we have raised, you may not find answers right away. It may not be immediately apparent who your elders are. You may have to look around. Where do you begin? Start by considering your grandparents and even your parents. How can you involve them in your lives?

You may not have any living grandparents in the area. However, it is highly likely that someone's grandparents live in your community. Invite them in. Tell them what you're doing. Embrace them and their wisdom. Do not force this relationship; let it happen naturally, by encouragement.

Most importantly, don't forget to pray that God will bring wise elders into your life. When our children were in the pre-teen years we did not have elders in our community, but this was a prayer request of ours. Soon, God brought into our lives two couples who filled that role perfectly.

The Power of Sanctifying Grace

We have talked about how the power of family identity and the power of community can help your family combat peer pressure. But it is the third power, the power of sanctifying grace, that will see your family through the middle and teen years.

Next to our computer screen is an Easter picture of our grandchildren. Ashley, the seven year old, has her arms stretched out across her siblings' and cousins' shoulders. At times, I (Gary) look at that picture and think and reflect on my own grandparents. It was nearly a century ago when, as children, each of them found the way of salvation in Jesus Christ. From those spiritual roots our family's Christian heritage began. As adults, my grandparents passed on the message to their children, who in turn passed it on to their own kids. We then taught our own children to believe in Jesus Christ, and they in turn are now actively passing on their faith to our grandchildren. By God's grace, Christianity has followed the blood line for five generations.

The duty of Christian parents to instruct their children in the knowledge of God cannot be achieved apart from His grace. As a parent, you want many things for your child. But the most important issue must be your child's salvation.

You may wonder what you can do to influence your child's decision. "Isn't salvation a personal issue?" you ask. "I certainly don't have the power to make it happen."

This is true. Salvation occurs, as the Bible says, by grace alone, through faith alone (Ephesians 2:8–9). Yet many parents wrongly conclude that dependency upon grace means they should relinquish all responsibility, or "let go and let God." The belief follows this logic: Why should parents bother to develop the moral character and conduct of their children if grace and salvation, the supreme goals, are not the direct result of moral training? As the Bible states, "Therefore...no flesh will be justified in His (God's) sight" by observing the law (Romans 3:20).

The simplest answer to that question is this: God requires the training of children. Proverbs 22:6 calls for us to "Train up a child in the way he should go." What is the result? "When he is old he will not depart from it." Ephesians 6:1–3 promises: "Children, obey your parents in the Lord, for this is right. 'Honor your father and mother,' which is the first commandment with promise: 'that it may be well with you and you may live long on the earth.'"

In his essays on the duties of a parent, the nineteenth century English cleric John C. Ryle warned parents to beware of the delusion that parents can do nothing for their children, that they must leave them alone, wait for grace, and sit still. Pastor Ryle understood well the importance of early training and passionately exhorted parents to participate in the communication of God's grace by opening the child's mind to, and directing his ways in, God's moral law. In this way, children are brought to a knowledge of God.

Of the various means by which God communicates His grace, three deserve our attention here. First, there is a *common grace* given to all mankind. Its benefits are experienced by the whole human race, without discrimination. For instance, God brings refreshing rain to the righteous and the unrighteous alike.

Second, there is *sanctifying grace*. God's grace flows to families through the sanctifying grace of believing spouses and parents. That is, when Mom and Dad have come to a saving knowledge of Jesus Christ, children receive the overflow of God's grace as it is poured out on their parents. The blessing is multiplied by each generation.

God's favor is extended through our obedience. If we want to claim for our children the blessings in God's Word, we must believe and be faithfully obedient to God's revelation. Without faith, we have no right to any blessings of promise. Without obedience, we cannot expect the favor of God nor the communication of His grace on our children or on our efforts. Grace is communicated to each household when parents stay vertically aligned with the Lord. As we are blessed, so will our children be blessed. This is the power of sanctifying grace.

Yet we know our children cannot live off of our blessings, but must obtain their own. This is done through the third means by which God communicates His grace—*regenerational grace*. This truth is basic to our entire presentation. No morality or conformity to the moral law can be acceptable to God, except that which is exercised in total dependence on Jesus Christ from a heart secured by Him. God delights in right behavior which arises from a right heart. Apart from receiving a new heart from the regenerating work of the Holy Spirit, no child has direct and personal access to God's grace.

Does this negate the divine call for parents to "Train up a child in the way of the Lord?" Most certainly not. It only serves to emphasize even more the parents' need to cooperate with the grace of God. A biblical view of grace doesn't call for parents to labor less. Rather, it calls them to labor fervently, all the while acknowledging their utter dependency upon God.

Seek diligently the salvation of your child, that he or she might enter into the fullness of God's power and influence and, out of a love response to God, serve Him whole-heartedly. In parenting, grace and labor are not enemies, but divinely appointed comrades in the work of the Lord. You cannot parent by your own strength and still achieve a godly outcome. Remember, let God through His grace do His part, while you through obedience do yours.

SUMMARY

The middle years is a time of change. It is the last phase of immaturity in the transition to moral maturity. Moral maturity is characterized by an increased capacity to direct one's own behavior by intrinsic values, to judge whether something is right or wrong, and to know why it is so. The middle years is also the time when gradual physiological changes begin to nudge children to a new awareness of themselves and of the opposite sex. This spawns a new era of significant peer relationships. New social stresses are placed on the child, and as a result, on the parent/child relationship.

This has always been so and will continue to be as long as man lives on this earth. God knew that and He did not leave us hopeless or helpless. Parents do make the difference when it comes to healthy parent/preteen and parent/teen relationships because Moms and Dads make choices every day. How obedient are you to God—every day? Have you been working on your family identity—every day? Who is in your family's community—every day? These questions must be evaluated honestly because the answers will have a tremendous impact on your family's future.

BRINGING IT HOME

1. When does peer pressure become negative?

2. What makes middle-years children and teens more vulnerable to peer pressure?

3. Define and explain identity association.

4. Explain why community is important to the successful rearing of children.

5. How important is the power of sanctifying grace, and how does it impact your household?

Chapter Seven

FATHER TO FATHER: BUILDING A TRUSTING RELATIONSHIP

Not long ago, our daughter Jennifer stopped by the house with two of our grandchildren. It was to be a quick visit to consult nurse Anne Marie about some running noses and feverish cheeks.

While Jennifer and her oldest daughter, Katelynn, found their way to grandma's office, eighteen-month-old Kara came to grandpa in his study. In need of hugs and kisses she wobbled over to my (Gary's) rocker, put out her hands, and uttered one word: "Up!"

I raised her first to my lap. Then, seeing she needed even more comforting, I brought Kara to rest on my chest and patted her as if she were a newborn. She snuggled into a comfortable position. I began to stroke her hair. Soon, she fell asleep, at peace with the world.

At that moment I thought, "How long has it been? Has it really been twenty-seven years since I held my own little girls like this?" Kara had come to me expectantly, her heart filled with innocent, unconditional trust. In her little mind there was no question about my love. There was no hesitancy, no doubt that I would bring her soothing comfort. At this age, Kara innocently believes that to receive love, all she has to do is open her arms and embrace it.

One day Kara will trade her boundless, innocent trust for a

more knowledgeable trust in human love and unconditional acceptance. She will learn through disappointment that the problem with trusting people is they are not always trustworthy. The degree to which her trust is violated in the future will determine whether she ultimately views relationships through a cloud of suspicion and doubt, or with confidence and clarity.

Your child, too, will face countless disappointments in the future. Friendships, work relationships, romantic entanglements—all provide opportunities for doubt. Your child's life will be filled with uncertainties. But you don't have to be one of them. Make sure your child has no reason to doubt you. Are you worthy of your preteen's trust? Does he or she know that no matter how fearful life becomes, Dad will be there to love and accept, help and guide?

All children are born with an inherent sense of trust in Mom and Dad. In the primary years, they believe everything we tell them, whether it is true or not. By our correct words and deeds we help them interpret life. Equally potent are our corrupt words and deeds. These, too, will shape their personal worlds. As surely as there is ink on this page, the innocent trust of early childhood will become metered and measured. It is during the middle-years that children trade their unquestioned trust in Mom and Dad for a more measured opinion about the trustworthiness of both. There is no point at which it is acceptable for us to grow lax and assume that our believability does not matter. It will always matter.

DEFINING TRUST

Trust is not a human emotion but a feeling of sustained confidence in a person, place, or thing. We step into an elevator because we believe the machinery to be capable of sustaining a lift. Every time we drive over a bridge, we demonstrate our trust in the security of the city's building codes. We go into surgery only after being assured of the skill and wisdom of the doctor holding the scalpel.

In much the same way, children trust their parents in many ways and for many things. They trust us for the mundane and important details of life. Because we continually provide them food, clothing, and shelter, they learn to trust us for their physical well being. They learn to trust our judgment on matters common to life: "The stove is hot. Stay away." "The wind is too strong. You'll lose your kite." They trust us to give them basic facts about life: "Milk spoils when it isn't refrigerated." "Water freezes at thirty-two degrees Fahrenheit." They learn to trust our wisdom: "Bad company corrupts good morals." "A soft answer turns away wrath." "Black ice is dangerous to walk on."

Perhaps the greatest role trust plays in parenthood is connecting our souls to those of our children. I speak now of the trust that binds together human relationships, especially family relationships. Think carefully about this next statement, for it qualifies everything that is to follow: *The quantity and quality of trust children have in us, as Fathers, is the only legitimate benchmark of our relationship with them.* Intimacy, the soul of human relationships, cannot be present if trust is absent or in doubt. Think back to the statements in the previous paragraph. Does your middle-years child trust you to provide him or her simply with sustenance, facts, and judgments? Or does he or she trust you as a person?

All children have basic needs. They need to know that they are loved, that they belong, and that they are accepted for who they are. For a child, trust is the bridge that links his need to know that he is loved with an understanding of being loved, his need to know that he belongs with a sense of belonging, and his need to be accepted with the knowledge that he truly is accepted. This is where we fathers come in. Dads are bridge builders. Without the bridge of trust, children have no point of relational connection back to the family.

How important is being connected? Extremely important. This is because the family provides a place for learning about meaningful relationships. This is where a child can be vulnerable without fear and where he can test his strengths, weaknesses, and limits. Through his or her family, a child begins to develop an understanding about the world. The meaning of life comes into perspective. Researchers have found that adolescents who feel connected to their parents and siblings are less likely than their peers to suffer from emotional distress, experience suicidal thoughts and behaviors, exhibit violent behavior, smoke cigarettes, drink alcohol, or use drugs. They perform better in school, enjoy deeper relationships, and are well adjusted. This sense of being connected occurs when each member of the family understands and accepts that he is part of something bigger than himself—his family. But before this can happen, there must be trust between family members. Middle-years children and teens who do not trust their parents cannot be connected to Mom and Dad.

As you think about the middle years, consider the role trust plays in your relationship. The bottom line is this: If your child cannot trust you, childhood peers will shape his or her future. How can you build a trusting relationship with your son or daughter? It won't just happen, but there are some practical things you can do to aid the process. Here are some relationship-building ideas to help you develop your relationship with your middle-years child.

Cultivate a Sense of Family Identity

If you want to build a trusting relationship with your middle-years child, start by cultivating attitudes that lead to a strong sense of family identity. In chapter 6 we defined this as the mutual acceptance by family members of your identity as a group and the values to which you ascribe. Family identity is based on trust, acceptance, and a growing loyalty between members. It is a significant factor in the life of every child, including your preteen. Even negative peer pressure is greatly minimized when a solid family identity is established.

A Christ-centered family identity is one in which family members are devoted to one another as Christ is devoted to His church. This devotion results in relationships that are based on trust and the acceptance of each family member as an individual, as well as loyalty to the family as a unit. These virtues of trust and loyalty are seen not just in family members' feelings and attitudes—but also in their actions.

In our home, family ties were never optional. Our children knew without question that God put us together for the purpose of representing Him to the world. Consistent loyalty to our family values sealed our identity as a unit. Even today, whether together or apart, we are committed to our family's standards. That attitude makes us mutually accountable. Each person knows the team is counting on every family member to stay committed to the code of ethics that represents us.

Verbalize Your Commitment to the Family

To speed up the process of bringing cohesiveness to your family, Dad, you must be assertive in leading your family. You cannot be a mere spectator, observing your wife's efforts to hold the family together. You must be an active leader and participant in the process.

When Dad is excited and encouraged about the family, children feel the same way. When he is silent about the family, the question lingers in their minds: Does he really care about us? You may think that by not talking, you are not communicating anything to your kids. Not so. With your silence you communicate a great deal: disinterest, or worse, fatherly disapproval or rejection.

This is why we urge fathers to verbalize their pleasure and excitement with their family. While driving in the car or sitting around the dinner table, encourage your family by making statements such as, "This is really a terrific family." "I am so thankful the Lord put us all together." "You kids have such a great Mom." As you talk about the family, you gain credibility in your role as the head of the home. Your child's confidence in you grows as he or she sees that Dad is on board.

When fathers cultivate family identity, they aid in the process of trust-building. The two go hand-in-hand. To nurture a strong family identity, fathers must weave trust into the fabric of each relationship.

Demonstrate Ongoing Love for Your Wife

The marriage relationship is the stage upon which the performance of trust is acted before your child's watchful eyes. Make no mistake: your son or daughter is observing you closely. And what he or she sees can have a tremendous impact, for the love and nurture you give your wife will help elevate your preteen's level of trust in you. Children thrive on the demonstration of love between parents. They need to feel confident that Dad is tremendously in love with Mom. A father can be wonderfully involved with his children—hiking, fishing, skating, taking walks, and helping with homework—but still nullify the results of his efforts if he does not continually cultivate a love relationship with his wife. Loving your wife is a prerequisite to building trust with your children.

In the New Testament, Jesus refers to marriage as a spiritual and physical union of which God Himself is the author (Mark 10:9). He also uses the institution to represent His deep and abiding relationship to the Church. In His para-bles, Jesus continually draws illustrations based on the insti-tution of marriage and specifically refers to the wedding feast four times (Matthew 22:2, 25:1; Mark 2:18–19; and Luke 5:34). Jesus affirms the one-flesh relationship as the heart of marriage. This is reaffirmed by the apostle Paul in Ephesians 5:31.

When the marriage relationship is made beautiful, what impressionable child would not desire to share in its joy? When two are beautifully as one, what child would not seek the comforts of Mom and Dad's togetherness? A strong mar-riage provides a haven of security for children of every age, including preteens. Children who are confident in their par-ents' love for each other fare better in life than those who are left wondering about Mom and Dad's commitment to each other. That is why one of the greatest gifts a father can give to his children is the ongoing demonstration of love for his wife. Here are two practical suggestions to consider.

Practice "Couch Time"

Strong families are built on strong marriages. Children delight in the visible demonstration of Mom and Dad's love for one another. One way this occurs is when husband and wife have a set time to commune with each other, in front of the kids. We call this "couch time."

When you and your wife arrive home at the end of the day, take fifteen minutes to sit on the couch with each other. Talk and enjoy each other's company. Explain to your chil-dren the importance of there being no unnecessary interrup-tions. Tell them this is a special time for Dad and Mom. Dad, explain that you will play with them later, but that time with their mother comes first. Every child wants to know his or her world is safe and secure. That reassurance begins with

Mom and Dad's relationship. Regular couch time between you and your wife provides a visual demonstration of your togetherness.

Have a Date Night

If you had a weekly date night with your spouse before your children were born, and if you have let that practice drop in the years since, resume that practice now. Let friends or relatives watch your kids or hire a trustworthy baby sitter.

If you have never had a date night, it is time to start having one. You need one. Your wife needs one. Your child needs you to have one. Your date does not have to be expensive, nor does it have to involve a late evening. The point is that you and your wife will be spending time together. Don't give in to the lie, "Our child won't be ok at home without us." Your child needs time with you, but he or she does not require your continual presence. The marriage relationship is the starting point of security for children.

Understand Your Child's Private World

If you want to find out what is going on with your middle-years child, you need access to his or her inner private world. Every person lives in three worlds—public, personal, and private. The public world includes much of the time we spend away from home (e.g., work and social activities) and allows us to keep relationships at a safe distance. Our personal world includes time spent with friends and relatives. In such settings, we are more relaxed and vulnerable.

But it is in our private world that we can be bold one moment and fearful the next. We can feel overwhelmingly discouraged or gleefully sing songs from the heart. We can be anxious or at peace with life. It is a place of personal thoughts, big wishes, and hopeful dreams. Our private world is the most secret of all places. No one can visit our private world without an invitation, for our private world takes place on the inside. Children have a private world that is constantly changing and developing during the middle years. Fathers need to be particularly sensitive to this world.

There is an interesting phenomenon with children called the "open window" that is often missed by parents who are too busy. Open windows are moments in time when your children will invite you in to their private world. These may happen when you're going on a walk with them, putting them to bed, or sitting in front of the fireplace, enjoying the warmth of the fire. Unexpectedly, children open up the window of their heart to invite you in.

On one occasion, I was putting our daughter Amy to bed, gently stroking the back of her head, and asking her how her day had gone at school. Suddenly she asked me, "Daddy, do you think I'm pretty? Do you think anyone else thinks I'm pretty?" At that moment, she was taking a risk with her dad. She was trusting me with the treasures of her heart.

When your child is willing to share the issues of his or her heart, you must seize the opportunity. When your preteen invites you into his or her private world, you must listen with your heart as well as your head. Although there are no guarantees in parenting, this statement comes close to being a certainty: If you can prove your trustworthiness during the vulnerable moments in the middle years, your son or daughter will come to you when he or she is older and facing life's challenges in the teen years. Your child will not forget you in times of need.

A father can establish a trusting relationship in the secret places of his child's heart, but he can destroy it there as well. That is why it is critical that you respect your child's private world.

Give Your Child the Freedom to Fail

Giving your child the freedom to fail almost sounds un-American. In our country, we love winning. At times, I wonder if this love has caused us to abandon our perspective and appreciation for what we can learn from losing. It is a crippling thing for a young, creative mind not to have the freedom to fail in front of Dad. Tell your child: "Anything worth doing well is worth doing poorly for a time." Reassure him or her that failure is acceptable, as long as he or she makes an honest effort. Your child needs to know that you view his or her failures as the first steps to success.

A father's wrong attitude toward failure can prevent his children from stretching themselves to their full potential. Imagine a child who is afraid to fail in front of his father because he senses Dad is not going to be pleased with him or fears that his father will not love him as much if he does not succeed. This child makes the status quo his standard. He will not develop the full range of talents and abilities God has given him. He would rather hold back, achieving only enough to get by, than face Dad's lukewarm reaction or angry dissatisfaction if he fails. Each time such an interaction occurs, the relationship slips back another notch.

Your children want you to be pleased and proud of them. If you continually respond to their failure with negative, sarcastic, or hurtful statements, rather than turning the situation into an opportunity for encouragement, you will do nothing to build trust.

Fathers must look at failure with an eye to the future, realizing that vulnerable moments of learning often accompany times of failure. In the Ezzo household, when our children failed—either in an achievement or a relationship—Anne Marie and I attempted to help them find the secret blessing. We often said, "Do you realize the number of adults who have not learned the lesson the Lord allowed you to learn today? Do you realize how many people live foolishly because they lack the wisdom you now possess?" Those were not words of condemnation or correction, but of encouragement. They were not meant to dismiss the pain of failure, but to help our kids see that out of defeat can come a victory they never expected. We knew they would be tested again in a similar fashion, and when that day came they would be ready to face it with wisdom. They would then turn failure into victory. And when that victory came, Dad (and Mom) would be there with praise.

We also used Scriptures to teach our children in the midst of trials and failure. Romans 5:3–4, Romans 8:28, and James 1:2–3 are passages we read and explained to our kids in such times. You, too, can use times of failure to instill biblical wisdom. Teach your child about the trials of the Old Testament character Joseph (Genesis 37:1–50:26) and how his right response to each trial allowed God to exalt him.

Your middle-years child needs to know that you also have failed and can share in his or her feelings of hurt and disappointment. Your preteen needs to be assured that your parent/child relationship is based on neither failure nor success. Please note: It is not the fear of failure itself that holds a child back, but the fear of failing *someone*. Often that someone is Dad. You must give your child reason to trust in a father who will remain loving and accepting when he or she fails.

Encourage Your Child

There is a big difference between an encouraging remark and an encouraging father. Real encouragement flows out of a relationship. It's more than a word now and then—it's your smile, expression, and very presence that communicate encouragement. Fathers need to be a source of encouragement because encouragement builds trust. Here are some practical activities for fathers to use to show encouragement to their children.

Dad's Little Notes

I often wonder how many young fathers wish their dads had written them just one note—something simple and encouraging. Something that ended in three little words: "I love you." It doesn't take much effort to occasionally put a little note in your child's lunch box. How much time does it take to write something like that? How much meaning can it have to your child? During the course of working with parents, we received the following short letter which demonstrates the potential such notes have to impact kids.

> Dear Gary and Anne Marie,
> I am writing to thank you and testify to the truth you imparted to us during last month's conference. I brought my husband to the seminar with the hope that he would be more willing to take a positive role in fathering if he heard things straight from you.
> A few days after we returned home, we were talking about fathers leaving notes for the child instead of Mom. (Something I had been doing for a few months.) My husband agreed to put a note in the lunch box of our eldest boy, who is now seven years old. The next morning the note was written with instructions to place it in the box, which I did. It was just a simple note saying, "Hope you have a nice day at school. See you when I get home. Love, Dad."
> Upon our son's arrival home, he handed me his lunch box as usual. When I opened it, the note was there. He obviously hadn't seen it so I said, "You missed something in your lunch box today." He took

the note and read it, and then, before me, my son broke down and wept. I hugged him and waited a few moments, then asked why he was crying. He replied, "I didn't realize Dad loved me that much." How can I ever thank you enough for such a priceless moment in the life of our child?

The time invested by this father was probably thirty seconds, but the impact of his thoughtfulness cannot be measured. The older the child, the more he or she needs to hear from Dad in writing. Take time to write your children a letter at least once a year. Sign it, seal it, and mail it. Your child will quietly realize the letter he or she holds is from a man unlike any other in the world—Dad. Letters from their friends may eventually get thrown out, but Dad's letters get safely put away. And in the future, during those discouraging moments or perhaps on lonely days, those notes come out again and again, bringing the reader an assurance of at least one certainty—Dad's love.

We also recommend that fathers sign family Christmas and birthday cards. It doesn't matter how illegible your penmanship might be. There is something very special about knowing Dad took the time to endorse the warm thoughts enclosed in the envelope. Children don't usually question Mom's commitment to the family, but such gestures confirm Dad's devotion. Wonderful memories result when Dad takes the time to compose special notes and sign cards.

Take your child's need for encouragement seriously. What may not be a big issue to you may be a major issue to your preteen. In the process of growing up, you have certainly experienced many of life's disappointments. You know from hindsight that you made it through and everything turned out fine. But your child doesn't know that. Many times a father underestimates a child's sense of urgency. What may seem trivial to you may be insurmountable to your son or daughter. Listen for the cues. Realize there will be some matters of major importance packaged in an insignificant statement. Seize the opportunity to encourage your child through his or her difficulties by imparting your experience and wisdom.

Routinely Embrace Your Child

Within the family, a gentle hand, a tender hug, a pat on the back, and a goodnight kiss all communicate intimacy in a relationship. To hold and be held communicates vulnerability and closeness that is reserved for trusting members of a family.

In our family, Anne Marie is the primary hugger. She came from a non-hugging family and vowed that our family would be different. It was. As a family when we greeted in the morning, we hugged. Before going out the door, we hugged. Just before bed, we hugged. We were devoted huggers, though we did not realize at first the emotional benefits of physical touch.

There is something very special about Dad's arms. Mom's arms are comforting, but Dad's arms are secure. Neither time, age, nor gender should limit a father's touch. Our children are never too old to be kissed, hugged, or held—never. Even as a full-grown man, I would give anything to be held one more time by my own dad, who passed away in 1972. I fear for the vast number of families whose fathers still have the opportunity to hold their children but don't.

Holding your child does more than provide security. It meets special emotional needs that one day will be met by your child's mate. This is particularly critical for fathers of daughters who are beginning to blossom into womanhood. Many dads unconsciously begin to back away physically when their daughters reach this stage in life. This is most painful for the girl who not only has to cope with her changing body, but also the devastating loss of Dad's physical affection.

Your daughter is still your little girl. She still needs hugs and kisses. If you fail to communicate your love through your touch, you will leave behind a yearning heart that can be taken captive by anyone willing to give it attention. Don't leave your child open to the affections of the wrong person. Hold your preteen and don't ever stop.

Build Your Family on God's Word, Not Human Wisdom

Trust cannot be separated from truth. Jesus said, "Your word is truth" (John 17:17). All the practical helps listed above are useless if a father is like the foolish man who builds his house upon the sand (Matthew 7:26–27). For when the storms of life sweep in and pound on your relationship, will anything be left after they pass? Without biblical truth, the family has no ultimate meaning or direction.

Parenting is a discipleship relationship in which truth passes from one generation to another. Without the truth of God's Word, there is the potential that a child can be spiritually lost. What is the father's mandate? To rightly reflect the truth of God, to develop a relationship of trust with his children based on that truth, and to communicate with his sons and daughters the biblical message of salvation through Jesus Christ.

DEALING POSITIVELY AND PROACTIVELY WITH SEXUAL CHANGES

Dads, the principles we've discussed so far are vitally important to relationships with both daughters and sons. But, in order to build trusting relationships with our kids, we must go one step further. As we have already discovered, we must be trustworthy, cultivate a sense of family identity, demonstrate an ongoing love for our wives, understand our children's private world, give our kids the freedom to fail, encourage them, routinely embrace them, and build our families on God's Word. Yet we must also proactively talk with our children about the sexual changes that are taking place within their bodies. If we do not, our kids will seek answers to their questions from other sources.

Because of this, Anne Marie and I encourage both Moms and Dads to have "the talk" with their children. It is best if fathers speak to sons and mothers to daughters, although in some single-parent families this is not always possible. In such cases, a loving aunt, uncle, grandparent, or family friend may step in, or you may sensitively approach the issue with your opposite-sex child. Either way, the following principles apply. We do recommend, however, that whenever possible, parents keep such education along gender lines. In the next chapter, Anne Marie will share with mothers how they can approach this subject with their daughters. Right now, I will finish this chapter by giving some basic advice on how to tackle this challenging subject with sons.

WORDS TO A SON

We must never forget that as fathers, we play an important part in the shaping of both our sons' and daughters' emotional and sexual development. To that end, physical touch—Dad's warm embrace and powerful hugs—should be extended to both daughters and sons.

Your preadolescent children need more than a hug, however. They also need an education about their changing bodies. As I have already stated, in the case of sons it is best that a father communicate this information.

Human sexuality is one of the most complex of all

human emotions, and there is much more to preparing your prepubescent son than communicating biological facts. I firmly believe that biological details need a relational and moral context if they are to have any real meaning to our children. But what our society is offering today is something far less than moral or relational. The exploitation of young minds for commercial gain encourages premature and distorted views of sexuality. This is certainly true in the case of boys. James Bond is offered as the ideal of masculinity—free to enjoy every woman who comes along, without any sense of commitment.

Can a father counter influences such as this? Yes, he can—by teaching and modeling for his son what it means to respect, honor, and appreciate the tenderness of womanhood. The extra effort we demonstrate and the many gestures of kindness we show our wives indelibly set in the minds of our sons a pattern of thinking and behavior that provide a context in which their sexual awareness can grow. If we as fathers don't do this, society will.

While girls' needs during puberty are generally addressed in helpful detail within every corner of society, boys' needs are often skimmed over with a few generalizations. "Boys are tough; they adjust just fine," we hear people say. The resulting impression is that girls are somehow more complex than boys. On the contrary—it takes great skill and insight to figure out what's going on in an eleven-year-old boy's head and body.

Because boys do not experience anything that signals the sudden onset of puberty (such as menstruation), many fathers feel no sense of urgency to talk with their sons about the changes about to occur in their bodies. Add to that the fact that boys are usually two years behind girls in physical and social development, and it's easy to see why often "the talk" never takes place. But some talking is necessary.

Puberty signals more than a change in voice or gangly growth; it signals the entrance into sexual maturity. Some amount of education is required; however, what a boy needs most is a sympathetic, knowledgeable, open, and trustworthy father who is eager and willing to answer his questions.

At the same time, a dad should not stand back and wait for his son to take the initiative with questions regarding sexuality, for a boy of this age likely feels some level of perplexed embarrassment over the changes he is beginning to experience. He may feel shame, or that surely he is the only boy his age thinking and feeling the way he does. As a result, he may internalize his questions, thoughts, and feelings and attempt to struggle through them alone.

For these reasons, it's vital that dads take loving initiative during their sons' middle years to give them some advance understanding of what they're likely to experience. Just as every father/son relationship is unique, so will be the various conversations between you and your son. Every father must decide to what extent he will communicate specific details and how explicit he will be. I do recommend that all such conversations be calm, positive and reassuring, and communicated in a manner that will assure them that 1) God designed sexuality, 2) that it is good, and 3) that it is part of His wonderful plan to help boys grow into responsible men and loving husbands.

Actively seek God's guidance in every aspect of these father/son talks, for your boy is going to face daunting inner struggles. Will you initiate conversation about self-sexual stimulation? Will you dialogue about the intense tingling and stiffness that comes on a young man, sometimes at the most awkward times? Will you coach him in dealing with peer pressure, media stimulation, and his own sensual fantasies? Will you discuss the changes he will experience physically, such as the growth of body hair; a cracking and deepening of the voice; and spurts of growth?

Every father must decide exactly how much information to impart, and when to do so. This decision will be based on family history, the peers with whom your child associates, the social and moral environments surrounding your preteen, the temperaments of both you and your child, and your middle-years child's age. Every family is different, and so is every child. Understand, therefore, that "more" information is not necessarily "better" information, but some information must be provided.

The decision of how and what to share is yours. But whatever you choose, it is imperative that you communicate to your son that he is not alone. Make sure he understands that he is not the only one to experience these sensations. Assure him that he is in good company, that all boys his age are in fact experiencing the same feelings and tensions.

Locker Room or Bathroom?

As we have already mentioned, there are many external changes taking place in your child during the preteen years. Usually around the age of ten or eleven for boys, body changes require you to give your child an education in grooming.

Let's start with a basic issue: deodorant. Friends of ours with four sons, two in the middle years, shared that one day they realized the family bathroom was beginning to take on the odor of a locker room. That was a clear sign that it was time for their eldest son to learn about personal hygiene.

This is a situation that must be handled sensitively. An off-hand suggestion such as, "Kid, you don't smell so good," has the potential to evoke emotions of shame and embarrassment in a child. So what is the best way to introduce something as basic as the need for deodorant? To begin with, dads must recognize that there is no need to be blunt or unkind. Statements such as "You stink. Start using some deodorant under your arms," or "I can smell you a mile away. It's time for the stick," threaten the security and trust we talked about earlier in this chapter. (Those also will be the words your children will use on their siblings.)

Sensitively educate your son about such matters. Explain the circumstances of physical maturity, including the fact that new sweat glands develop as bodies grow. Help your preteen understand that he is not alone in this change and that it happens to everyone during preadolescence. Explain how sweat attaches to our skin, underarm hair, and clothes and why bathing, changing clothes, and using deodorant are important daily habits. You may be able to take advantage of seeing a deodorant commercial by making a comment such as: "That guy on the commercial is using roll-on deodorant. That's what I use, and at the rate you're growing, Son, you're going to need your own soon." Then, you can sit back and wait for the questions to arise. Don't worry if none come right away. Your son may simply be processing the comment. In time, however, both his curiosity and need to know will increase.

The practice of self-care and personal hygiene is second nature to adults. For children, however, this is not the case. They must be taught, and gently. As physically maturing children detect new smells and experience other bodily changes, they often feel an overwhelming sense of self-consciousness. Reassure your son that adults have the same problem with perspiration, but they know how to take care of it—just as he will learn to do.

Indoctrinating your son into life after puberty goes far beyond the knowledge of how to use deodorant, however. You must also deal with the disparity between what he wants to know and needs to know about the new and powerful feelings that are beginning to surge through his body.

As with all conversations in the Christian home, any dialogue about sexuality must take into account the truths and precepts in God's Word. Explain to your son that according to God's timetable, his body will awaken to entirely new sensations that are good and pleasurable and given by the Lord. Instill in him the knowledge that these feelings are sacred and their full expression must be realized only within the context of marriage.

As you discuss with your son his growing sexuality, share with him the truth that he, along with all other boys around his age, will soon have the God-given biological capacity to bring about human life. Emphasize that with that capacity comes a great responsibility to properly manage these new feelings and drives that come from deep within. Explain that this is made possible by keeping his heart and mind pure, focusing on God-centered thoughts, and building friendships with other kids who are also committed to living godly, moral lives.

Above all, Dad, you must be available to your son. Sometimes you will initiate the conversation or encourage him to bring questions to you. At other times, your son will bring up a subject. But always, your middle-years child must have the confidence that you will encourage and respect this area of his developing masculinity.

SUMMARY

Clinical textbooks often define healthy parent/child relationships as a mutual interaction between adult and child in which the adult provides the child with affection, stimulation, and unbroken continuity of care. But that type of generic definition is misleading and falls short. As we have already seen, a healthy parent/child relationship is all that and more. It is a relationship that is characterized by mutual harmony and respect among each of its members. It is the breeding ground where trust and forgiveness are learned, loyalty is experienced, and security is realized.

This type of family interaction doesn't just happen. There are family dynamics that make them so. Healthy marriages, trusting relationships, strong family identity, respected inner worlds, and security in each other's friendship are but a few. As you move forward with your middle-years child, don't forget to take with you the fundamentals of great families.

Remember also, your responsibility to talk with your son about sexual changes that will be occurring in his body. Both the information given and approach taken will vary from father to father, but all dads must make sure there is an open line of communication, and all sons must know they can talk to Dad—about *anything*.

BRINGING IT HOME

1. In family relationships, what does trust connect?

2. What is "couch time" and what purpose does it serve?

3. Explain the meaning of this statement: The quantity and quality of trust your children will have in you is the only legitimate benchmark of your relationship with them.

4. Why should parents, and especially fathers, verbalize their commitment to their family?

5. Explain the open-window phenomenon.

Chapter Eight

MOM TO MOM: GETTING READY FOR CHANGE

S hortly after her eighth birthday, Frannie came to her mother and asked with a serious look on her face: "Mom, Debbie at school says that her sister Gretchen got a period. When I asked her what she meant, she started laughing at me. She said I was a baby and wouldn't understand until I was older." Frannie's brow furrowed. "What did she mean by that, Mom?"

Frannie's mother gazed at her daughter. "Let's sit down and talk about it," she said sensitively. But in the back of her mind, she wondered: Is it too early to be talking about this with my daughter? Or am I starting too late?

It's not uncommon for a mother to feel some confusion at this stage of parenting. During the preteen years, many new situations will come up, and previously unimportant issues will now need to be addressed. Some relate to physical changes; others concern emotional and social development. But one thing remains consistent from family to family: changes are coming, and Mom needs to be prepared.

WHERE DOES A MOTHER BEGIN?

Where does a mom start as she sees her son or daughter on the brink of adolescence? That's a question I (Anne Marie) asked many years ago, and it's a question you may very well be asking today. As mothers, we enter into our children's middle years with a fairly good track record of knowing the clothes to purchase, the meals to plan, and the activities in which we should allow our kids to participate. Up to this point, we have been carrying out the general management of our children's lives. We led; they followed.

But all that changes as your child enters the middle years. This phase of life presents a challenging transition not only for your son or daughter, but for you. Because mothers become so proficient at managing, changes that involve letting go and stepping back can be difficult to make. The woman who has dedicated herself to the mothering role may find the prospect of growth changes to be potentially traumatic.

As our children move further and further away from our direct maternal supervision, we might feel that our influence is being devalued. Understandably, this is why some moms feel threatened by their children's emergence into the middle years. The son or daughter who needed us for everything a few short years ago is now managing his or her own life and forming opinions about the world. This includes opinions about the need and value of mom's supervision.

Remember Jesus' words: "Let not your heart be troubled" (John 14:1, 27). As a mother and grandmother, I have often seen that what we fear about change usually doesn't come to pass. Eventually we adjust to the spreading of our children's wings. We come to appreciate new sides of ourselves and learn that we are more adaptable then we thought. We have already acknowledged that your middle-years child is a changing human being. As a mom, you must flex with that change and grow in God's grace as it occurs.

THE VALUE OF FAMILY

During this time, it's important that you remember how important you are in your child's world. Yes, outside influences are becoming more of a factor. But there is still no greater influence in a child's life than that of his or her family. It is within the family that children develop a sense of who they are, and it is by their parents' compass that they find the direction in which they will start out in life. How well, or how poorly, a child adjusts to adolescence is often the result of how well his or her parents adjusted to the many transitions found in the middle years.

Although a family will share a common roof, meals, and love, no two members of the family relate in exactly the same fashion. Your preadolescent, for example, relates to "Mom and Dad" as a unit differently than he or she relates to either parent alone or when in a group of siblings. You, as a parent, also treat that child differently when you are alone together than you do when your other children or spouse are present.

As your child moves through preadolescence, both the mother/child and father/child relationship will take on new significance. Daughters look to their mothers to model their future role of womanhood. Fathers, in turn, provide a sounding board upon which girls can test their femininity. For example, your daughter may love to go shopping with you, but it is Dad she runs to, to show her new outfit. She does this for a reason greater than just showing off her purchase. She is measuring his response as a type of masculine gauge. "What does Dad think?" often translates into "What will boys think about me in this dress?"

Parent/child relationships are also highly significant to preadolescent boys. Sons need their mothers to remain the emotional cushion they fall back on when life gets tough. While a preteen boy may not physically crawl up into Mom's lap for comfort anymore, he will continue to seek that comfort in less direct ways. You may see evidence of this in your son's need for compliments or approval, or the desire simply to be near you while you are cooking dinner or going about your daily tasks.

Preteen boys need their fathers to mentor them on their journey into manhood. Your husband's treatment of you during your son's impressionable preadolescent years has a profound influence on that child's understanding of, and behavior toward, girls.

PREPARING FOR SURVIVAL

We all bring different personal experiences and backgrounds to our mothering. Yet there are certain aspects of womanhood that are constant. The desire to nurture drives us to equip our sons or daughters to care for their basic personal needs and to provide a working model of what it means to run a home. Do not assume such skills will naturally be learned without your influence.

Preparing your children to be self-sufficient is a process. When my own children were quite small, I set several "survival goals" for them. I would recommend this practice to all young moms. By the time each of my daughters reached thirteen years of age, I wanted her to have a working knowledge of how to run a home. That included the basics of shopping for food and clothing, preparing simple meals, doing laundry, cleaning the house, managing a budget, and even preparing Thanksgiving dinner. These are some of the survival goals I set for my children; you will certainly have your own list. As I worked with my daughters, however, my thought was simply this, "If something should happen to me, could the girls take care of themselves, and their dad?"

I did not wait until my children were on the verge of their teen years to begin the training. I had a proactive plan that began to take shape when they were very young. As the girls moved into the toddler years I began to teach them how to sort clothes and put them into baskets. They would often follow me to the washer and observe the process of putting the clothes inside and adding detergent. When it came time to hang out the clothes (yes, coming from New England, I actually hung up my clothes), the girls, upon instruction, would hand me the item to go on the line. As they grew, each girl learned how to fold clothes and eventually how to put them away. Did this all take extra time? Of course. But all training does.

I followed a similar procedure for each skill I wanted them to learn. For example, it was not uncommon for one of the girls to be found sitting on a stool in the kitchen as I cooked. They would observe my actions and, when they were developmentally able, place the ingredients into the mixing bowl. If necessitated by their age, I would hold their hand as we used the mixer or turned the mixture with a spoon. It was not until the girls were around ten years of age that I was fully confident I could let them use the stove.

Let me make one important clarification here: domestic duties are not just for girls. In the sphere of a mother's influence, sons should learn the same things daughters do. Practically speaking, that means boys learn to do laundry, vacuum, wash dishes, iron their own shirts, wash floors, and help Mom hang curtains. If you are the mother of a son, consider your future daughter-in-law. Every son is potentially a future husband. He is in training to be a responsible partner and a godly spouse.

You and your husband both have a responsibility to help your sons in this area. While more of the "teaching" or "training" may fall on your shoulders, it is his father's example your son will follow. If your husband demonstrates a willingness to help around the house as needed, your son will be much more likely to learn the same behavior.

The object is to set a goal and to walk your child—boy or girl—through the steps to achieve it. Whether that goal is having the skills to set a formal table, greet an honored guest, or cook a chicken, the process of learning should be initiated early. By the time your son or daughter is a teen, he or she should be ready to take over the household duties should the need arise. Once this level of readiness is reached, your child will also be prepared to feed, clothe, and care for him- or herself during the young adult years that lie ahead.

WORDS TO A DAUGHTER

From the beginning of time, mothers and daughters have shared a unique bond. While a son will break away and follow his masculine identity, a daughter will see herself as joined to her mother by love, feelings, gender, and the powerful ability to nurture and bear life with her own body. The impact of such knowledge is confirmed by one of the most significant events in her life, the beginning of menstruation. Although our daughters will have their own feelings related to estrogen and progesterone, their experiences draw our mutual sympathies and create an unspoken world of sisterhood.

A preadolescent girl's growth and development can become a source of anxiety and confusion. As thirteen-year-old Casey watched her dad swing, twirl, and wrestle with her seven-year-old sister, she sighed. Turning to her mom she said, "I wish I didn't have to grow up anymore." Casey wanted to put a halt to puberty changes. Unfortunately, her budding entrance to womanhood had put a stop to her father's familiar play-touch. (In our last chapter, Gary cautioned fathers not to physically back away from their developing daughters.) Now Casey is resistant to change. But this resistance is not the result of a misconceived idea about the process of maturing; it is the result of how her maturation is affecting other relationships.

PUBERTY

What is puberty, and when does a child reach it? Scientists tell us that puberty is a phase of physical development, a biological marker that signifies sexual maturity. It is triggered by the hypothalamus, a region located at the base of the brain that regulates the activity of the pituitary gland. The word puberty originates from two words, "growth" and "hairy." This refers to the development of pubic hair. Around eleven years of age for girls, pubic hair usually appears as the early phase of breast development begins.

As stated in chapter 2, hormonal changes in the endocrine system begin in children at approximately age seven, not twelve or thirteen, as commonly believed. Around nine and a half, hormonal changes trigger a prepubescent growth spurt in girls. By the time they reach fourteen, the average girl will have become twenty-five percent taller and almost doubled her body weight. It is no wonder that during this rapid growth period girls become more self-conscious about their personal appearance.

During this phase of growth my own daughters began to require more sleep at night, and after-school naps were not uncommon. The little cereal dishes of childhood were replaced with Mom-and-Dad-sized bowls. This increased appetite made glandular sense; the hypothalamus was signaling a need for more food so that the body could get enough energy to meet its growing demands. During the middle years, more than ever, moms need to provide nutritional meals and snacks and help their children avoid junk food.

Of all the changes that take place with your daughter during puberty, the onset of monthly menstruation creates the most anxiety. Menstruation is not a gentle, gradual, or leisurely transition. It is a spontaneous event that comes without advance warning from the body. One day your daughter simply discovers that she is bleeding. This occurrence can be a great source of fear. However, education can greatly reduce your daughter's apprehension and anxiety.

STEPS OF PREPARATION

How can you prepare your daughter for the changes that are about to come, especially for menstruation? Out of my experience as a nurse, childbirth educator, and most importantly, as a mother of daughters, I have gathered a few suggestions to help guide your efforts.

1. Realize you have competition.

Early in the Book of Genesis, we see examples of how God's plan for human sexuality has been twisted. Consider the two wives of Lamech (Genesis 4:19), the rape of Dinah (Genesis 34:2), and the harlotry of Timnah (Genesis 38:16). Clearly, the human race wasted no time in finding a way to pervert the "one man, one woman" design of Genesis 2:24.

Today, things are no different; our children live in a world of sexual deviancy. Your preteen is growing up in a day and age when sexuality is neither regulated within marriage, nor governed by Judeo-Christian values. Sex is a commodity for sale, and it does sell well. Prime time television exploits it, magazine advertisements profit by it, and young girls are told they can become glamorous by flaunting it. Public discourse is constantly bombarding our young children with sexual imagery that excites curiosity and stirs the fires within. This is the moral environment to which your message of purity will enter, and with which you must compete.

Your daughter knows her body is changing and that she is in the throes of an unaccustomed set of emotions and sensations. She also knows that sex has something to do with it all. You must prepare her for a life of uncompromising holiness and sexual purity in a world that finds such notions antiquated, distasteful, and dangerous.

2. Realize the context of your sexual message is already established.

No conversation about sexuality takes place in a vacuum. Everyday, in a number of ways, we communicate sexual messages and values to our sons and daughters. The way a husband and wife respond to each other at the close of the workday will carry a subtle message of sexuality. Do you and your husband kiss at the door? How long do you kiss? Do you hug? How tightly? How do you look at one another? When your parents come by for a visit, do you hug the same way with the same intensity, and kiss the same way in front of them as you do when they are not present?

Your attitude toward biblical modesty has a profound effect on your child's moral development because it sets the parameters of acceptable and unacceptable thinking. What you wear around the house (a sheer nightgown or a bathrobe) and what you watch on television are just two examples. Parental purity communicates family attitudes that ultimately provide your child with a frame of reference. Your children are watching you. Over time and in a deep way, you are leaving an impression about sexuality—yours and theirs. It is into this context that you begin to teach your daughters about the changes to come and what they mean physically and morally.

3. Realize Mom is the best person for the job.

During a break at one of our conferences, a mom came to me with an all-too familiar story. "Not long ago our niece, Christy, came to live with Bob and me. Not only was her parents' divorce traumatizing, but right in the middle of all of this emotional turmoil she started her period. I called my sister-in-law to find out how prepared Christy was. She told me

Christy learned everything she needed from this terrific book the school nurse provided the fourth grade girls. That book had been a substitute for "Mom's talk," and for Christy it was not enough.

If sex education, and especially a conversation about menstruation, was simply a matter of communicating biological facts, then a book *would* be enough. But female sexuality is much more complex. That is why a child's mind and heart both must be prepared.

This is one reason Gary and I are not in favor of preadolescent books that are written simply to educate children on the issue of puberty and sexuality. Such books often presuppose virtues to be present and active in the life of the young reader. Unfortunately, those virtues often are not there. Sex educators can anticipate neither the quantity nor the quality of moral training a home life has fostered. If the minds and hearts of children have not been prepared properly, even the most nobly conceived book can devastate a young mind by providing information the child is not ready to handle. A book of knowledge is not a good substitute for a mom with knowledge.

4. Realize there is a timing issue related to your talk.

The sharing of bio/sexual information with children is progressive. In truth, there is no such thing as a one-time chat with our daughters. Rather, we engage in a series of talks that culminate in a specific conversation about menstruation. Speak to your daughter with sensitivity, and always seek to preserve her dignity.

Dialogue between mother and daughter can begin around the age of nine. It was around that age that I began with my own daughters by hinting about issues of their development. By the use of the word *hinting* I do not mean I withheld information from the girls. I simply began to make reference to changes that were coming. For example, there came a time I bought deodorant for myself and, for the first time, for my daughter. When I got home, I gave her the product, asked her to put it away, and casually told her she was going to need it soon because her body was about to go through some changes.

This simple comment brought a simple question: "Why?" From that one question I was able to approach the topic of her change in a very nonthreatening manner. "One of the signs that you are maturing is the presence of underarm perspiration. That is why teenagers and adults use deodorant. It helps take care of the smell that comes with the sweat, so we are not offensive to other people. There will be more changes to talk about later, but for now put your deodorant away." That little conversation went a long way. It opened the door for questions, and gave me a jumping off point for our next conversation, which took place at around age nine and a half.

Some of my friends with daughters were more technical in their explanations. When the window of opportunity came, they first approached the subject by discussing how the hypothalamus and pituitary gland regulate the hormones that cause body changes. For these women, a more textbook-type approach worked best.

When my daughters reached nine and a half I was more direct than I had been before, but still discreet. I started to talk generally about Cassandra, a teenager at our church, remarking that she was beginning to blossom into a beautiful young lady. The kids admired Cassandra so she became a good role model for them. My conversation now included some specific details of how wonderful God made our bodies and explained in simple terms about hormones that cause girls like Cassandra to grow toward womanhood. I told them that like Cassandra, they too would soon begin to develop breasts, and I informed them that some hair would begin to appear in their pubic region.

My mother/daughter conversations about menstruation became more direct at around the time each daughter reached age ten. It was then I began to notice the early signs of their maturing, including the first stages of breast development and pubic hair. These conversations took some planning on my part. I wrote to one of the many feminine hygiene companies and requested a "starter packet" that could be used to generate discussion with my daughter. The package I received was very helpful. If you take this same approach, however, I would urge you to first review the box and its contents. Some information may not be appropriate for your daughter. All she needs at this age is basic information about the anatomy as it relates to her menstrual cycle and her personal hygiene.

For a young girl, perhaps the most confusing aspect of menstruation is the role blood plays in the process. Why blood? What is the function and purpose of it? At some time during one of your mother/daughter conversations, you should help your child put the process of menstruation into perspective by answering these questions.

In Leviticus 17:11a we read: "For the life of the flesh is in the blood." In the truest biological sense, there are life-sustaining properties within blood. Add to this understanding the following truth: God has ordained that children shall be conceived and grow within the womb, or uterus. Tell your daughter that once a month, a woman's body places life-sustaining nutrients into the womb. These nutrients are contained within the blood. If no child is conceived that month, the blood with all its special "food" will be passed out of the body. Explain that this begins what is commonly referred to as menstruation, or a period.

As a mother, you will, of course, regulate your conversation and determine how extensively you will answer questions, based on your daughter's age, moral and sexual awareness, and her ability to process all that she is hearing. But at some point, this information will be helpful. If your child never knows the answer to the question, "Why blood?" the entire process will continue to be nothing more than a mysterious, confusing nuisance she must live with every month.

Early in your first conversations you might hear from your daughter, "Oh, I know all about periods. Becky told me it happened to her sister at school." Do not let that statement go unchallenged. Follow it up with, "I'm sure you have a general knowledge about this, but do you know about ovulation, or the mild cramps that may accompany your period?" Ask questions. Do not end this conversation without understanding what she knows in contrast to what she thinks she knows.

It is also important that you not assume each daughter will receive the news in the same way. I had one daughter whose emphatic response was, "That's not going to happen to me!" To this, I gently responded, "Yes, in fact, whether you like it or not, this happens to all women. It is part of life, and you will adjust to these changes just as all women before you have adjusted." Her sister received the same talk, but this daughter's response was one of great anticipation and excitement about growing up. There was no right or wrong response in these two examples, but both need to be directed and understood.

I issue one final warning: Do not feel obligated or pressured into sharing sexual information beyond the basics of menstruation. Your daughter at this age does not need to know about the intimate details surrounding the act of marriage. What needs to be said on that subject will come later as she moves into moral maturity and preparation for marriage.

Certainly, answer whatever questions she has, but keep the answers age-appropriate and related to the changes in her body.

5. Realize the importance off follow-up.

Keep in mind there will always be teaching opportunities, before and after menstruation starts. Television commercials serve as good starting points. If you and your daughter are together and you see an advertisement for a feminine hygiene product, use that opportunity to discuss the merits of that particular product in hopes of triggering further discussion about her menstruation. Once her cycle starts, help her understand that "normal" is what is normal for her. While many have a period every twenty-eight days, some go longer and some shorter. Make sure your daughter understands that irregular cycles, particularly initially, are not uncommon. That fact will allow you to speak further to the issue of preparedness and personal hygiene.

It is likely that conversations with your daughter will sooner or later lead to the question of Dad. "Does Dad know about these things?" asked one concerned twelve year old who was feeling a little embarrassed. We believe that fathers should be told when their daughters begin menstruation. Your husband needs to know, not because he will serve as an advisor in such matters, but because he must be made aware of the need to be sensitive to his daughter concerning the many changes about to take place physically and emotionally.

Girls feel more comfortable talking with mothers about the intimate details of menstruation and their developing bodies. Dad does not have to be part of this conversation, and usually he is not welcome. That is ok. Mothers have shared with me how their daughters recoiled at the thought of Dad's involvement in any conversation about menstruation. Young girls believe their fathers could not possibly understand these things. And they are right to some extent. Emotionally and experientially, most men are limited in the full appreciation of menstruation. Keep Dad informed and encourage him in his role as a loving and dedicated father. Continually remind him to hug her and affirm her developing femininity. But do not assume that he is an equal voice on this matter, one that she will appreciate hearing from. He is not.

Finally, when your daughter starts to menstruate, *do not* announce it at the dinner table, at the woman's Bible study at church, or to the neighbor next door. If you do that, you severely damage or destroy the trust and confidence your daughter has in you. There are enough challenges in a preadolescent and adolescent's life. Sharing facts about the beginning of her period will only complicate matters for her. Be sensitive to this. This is an issue between daughter and mother. Leave it there.

6. Realize that your daughter will have concerns.

Think back to the questions you had when you first learned about, or began, menstruation. You may or may not have brought your concerns to your mother. But you do want your daughter to be able to come to you.

In all likelihood, your daughter will have questions that reflect the very same concerns you had as a young girl. These concerns can be greatly reduced, if not completely eliminated, through proactive guidance. Here are five of the most common concerns young girls have regarding menstruation. By being aware of them, you will be able to more effectively support and understand your daughter during this difficult phase of life.

Concern #1: Everyone at school will know I'm having my period.

Your daughter's increased self-consciousness and heightened sensitivity to her own body trigger this concern. After she begins menstruating, she will notice that in addition to the increased perspiration that naturally occurs with the development of sweat glands, body secretions and the passing blood will also give off a slight odor. The solution, of course, is basic hygiene. Let your daughter know she will make it through her period without detection if she routinely changes her pads, takes daily showers, and when she is ready, considers the use of feminine hygiene products.

Concern #2: It can strike at any time.

It is frightening for a young girl to know that she may begin bleeding at any moment. You can help reassure your daughter by explaining the concept of cycles. While there are charted average norms, let your daughter know that menstruation cycles vary from woman to woman. Some women's cycles are twenty-four, twenty-eight, or thirty-two days. Others may be longer or shorter. Your daughter needs to understand that "normal" for her is whatever her cycle proves to be. Over time, she will establish regular and predictable patterns. Predictability then leads to the three "Ps": planning activities, preparing for surprises, and preventing accidents.

Concern #3: I will bleed to death.

Prior to the onset of menstruation, your daughter's only experience with bleeding has been related to injury. It is natural and logical for her to wonder how much blood can be lost before bleeding becomes life-threatening. Assure your child that while it may feel like she is losing a lot of blood, blood loss during menstruation is insignificant—usually less than two ounces—and is blood that God has designed to be lost. This is also the time to teach the importance of proper nutrition, which is essential for the body to maintain proper fluid balances, including the production of red blood cells.

Concern #4: It's going to hurt.

Menstruation cramps, mild to severe, are a fact of life. However, we live in a day and age when over-the-counter medication is available to help a woman through the first days of her period. Help your daughter understand her analgesic choices.

Also, please be aware that you have a profound influence on how your daughter responds to menstrual cramps. Remember, every woman responds to pain and discomfort differently. Be careful how you communicate your own experiences and responses. If you take to bed once a month, do not assume that your daughter's body will necessitate the same. On the other hand, if you are blessed with mild to no cramping, do not assume your daughter's physiology will grant her the same benefits.

Concern #5: I can't do anything or go anywhere during my period.

It is true that due to some discomfort, menstruation may lead to the occasional curtailment of a particular physical activity. However, menstruation in and of itself will not prevent your daughter from participating in gym class, swimming, or other sports and social activities that she enjoys. Reassure her that though some adjustments will need to be made, she can and will enjoy life just as much as she has before.

No matter how many helpful talks you have with your daughter, how many concerns you alleviate, or how conscientious you are as a parent, it is inevitable that she will experience some anxious moments. This cannot be avoided. However, you can ease your daughter's tension by nurturing an open, loving, and understanding relationship with her. It is your job, Mom, to communicate the facts as your daughter needs them; to be interested, sympathetic, and ready to help when called upon; and to demonstrate your confidence in her ability to face these incredible life changes. Above all, both you and your daughter's father must realize that menstruation is another middle-years transition she must experience. Through this rite-of-passage, she will leave behind the protected and sheltered world of childhood and begin a new journey to the privileges and responsibilities of womanhood.

SUMMARY

In the last chapter Gary spoke to the issue of trust. Trust involves keeping confidence, being sympathetic, and understanding. Trust involves friendship and constant affection. Once our daughters begin to blossom into womanhood, they need a good friend more than anything. In fact, they shift their friendship emphasis of a few years earlier from a friend as someone to play with, to a friend as someone to talk to and share life with. For this wonderful season of preadolescence and adolescence, mothers need to cultivate this type of friendship with their children.

BRINGING IT HOME

1. Define the new role Mom takes in the role of her middle-years child.

2. In your own words, explain the various changes experienced by moms and daughters, and the difficulties they raise.

3. When does a child reach puberty?

4. What is wrong with just giving your child a book about sexuality?

5. When should you begin to explain to your daughter about the changes taking place in her body? Why is it important to have progressive conversations, and not just a one-time talk?

Chapter Nine

COMMUNICATING EFFECTIVELY WITH YOUR MIDDLE-YEARS CHILD

Have you ever thought about how much we need God's wonderful gift of communication? Try to imagine living isolated from the world, without any way to communicate to others. How would you ever express "I love you" to your children or hear the words, "Thanks, Mom"?

We all need to be able to communicate effectively. You need to communicate with your spouse, your boss, your friends, and yes, your middle-years child. In turn, your son or daughter needs to communicate with you and with others in his or her world.

How are your preteen's communication skills developing? As family educators, we have observed that how a child communicates during the middle years is usually reflective of how he or she will communicate in adulthood.

You may think you already understand your child's communication style. But, as we have already seen, things tend to change dramatically during the middle years. For example, young Billy talked excessively from first through third grade. But he became more reserved during the middle years as he began to gain greater self-control in both speech and conduct. An opposite example of this change is Lindsey, who was shy in early childhood but gained the confidence to be a great communicator during the middle years.

Communication is an important part of relationships. Speaking and listening are God-given abilities that enable us to verbally express feelings, utter sound with meaning, and write words with intent.

God understands our need for communication. He, Himself, is a communicating and conversational God. The Scriptures are filled with examples of this. Adam and Eve heard the Lord in the garden. The child Samuel heard Him in the temple. Moses heard God speak from a burning bush. The list continues with hundreds of examples of the phrase "The Lord said" appearing in Scripture.

Not only does God speak, He listens. He listens to the cries of His people and hears their prayers. He's not only the creator of communication, He's the supreme example of its use. In contrast, all humans—Moms and Dads included—can benefit by brushing up on the use of such skills. We can learn to listen more attentively and speak more graciously.

All this is beneficial to us, but communication skills cannot make up for a lack of relational health. "Good communication" has become a catch-phrase in discussions about troubled marriages and struggling parents. While it is true that a lack of communication is usually a symptom of an unhealthy relationship, this does not mean that poor communication was the cause of the problem.

The possession of communication skills does not ensure that family harmony or healthy relationships will follow. Communication skills are not a substitute for values. What holds families together is the moral unity found within the soul of the family. Moral intimacy among family members has no substitute, no backup, no replacement. That's why we believe good speaking and listening skills are important parts of, but not a substitute for, healthy relationships.

We all know of great communicators who have little, if

any, relationship with their kids. Even worse, they may have children who desire no relationship with them. This only proves our point that good communication skills are not a substitute for good values. Knowing how to communicate with your spouse and kids is certainly important, but it is more important that you first learn to biblically love and live with your family. Unconditional love is the vehicle used to develop this rapport.

In this chapter, we will address the factors that influence healthy preteen and teen communication. But first we must understand the biblical ethics that govern how we speak and listen.

THE ETHICS OF COMMUNICATION

Creating and maintaining a climate of trust where our kids feel secure enough to communicate openly and honestly with us must be a high priority for parents living with middle-years children. Two important factors in establishing this climate are how we speak and how we listen.

As Christians, we turn to God for wisdom. The Bible shows us clearly that He does have an opinion on the ethics of communication. In a moment, we will lead you through some practical tools you can use to foster healthy communication with your child, but it is important to begin by considering what God says about the subject. Practical advice is meaningless if it is not anchored in the Word of God.

Speaking

The Book of Proverbs offers a number of important messages about our speech. In Proverbs 25:11 we learn of the importance of a timely message: "A word fitly spoken is like apples of gold." Proverbs 15:1 warns of our tone: "A soft answer turns away wrath, but a harsh word stirs up anger." Proverbs

16:24 speaks of the care we should take in selecting positive words: "Pleasant words are like a honeycomb, sweetness to the soul and health to the bones."

Scripture also tells us our integrity is demonstrated by our words: "But above all, my brethren, do not swear, either by heaven or by earth or with any other oath. But let your 'Yes' be 'Yes,' and your 'No,' 'No,' lest you fall into judgment" (James 5:12). This is an important reminder to us as parents; that our yes must mean yes, and our no must mean no. This is part of living with integrity and making sure we're upright in all our dealings with our kids.

Listening

The ethics of Scripture also govern listening. Proverbs 18:13 instructs us to listen to all facets of an issue before speaking: "He who answers a matter before he hears it, it is folly and shame to him." This is a key verse for parents. When the family has only small children, this isn't as much of a problem. But as the kids get older, Mom and Dad are often quick to make a judgment. Especially when we're in a rush, it's easy to interrupt our children and answer too quickly. We think we know what our kids are going to ask, but often our answer does not even come close to answering their true questions. God says such behavior is folly and a shame to us as parents.

Proverbs 18:17 teaches us not to listen to just one side of the story: "The first one to plead his cause seems right, until his neighbor comes and examines him." In cases of family, that "neighbor" could very well be a sibling.

Proverbs 1:33 charges us to listen to the voice of wisdom for our own safety: "But whoever listens to me will dwell safely, and will be secure, without fear of evil." And finally, we are instructed: "Let every man be swift to hear, slow to speak," and, as a result, "slow to wrath" (James 1:19).

SIX KEYS TO HEALTHY COMMUNICATION

One of the best ways we can encourage our middle-years children is through healthy, proactive communication. Good communication can prevent more conflicts than corrections can ever solve. Preadolescents and teens communicate their feelings much more readily than younger children, possibly because their vocabulary is more extensive. The words needed to reflect inner abstract feelings are now present and meaningful talk can take place. Take advantage of this opportunity. Now is the time to establish communication patterns that will help you avoid, and work through, conflict. You must learn how to talk so your kids will listen, and how to listen so your kids will talk.

Healthy communication serves as the vehicle that transfers our thoughts, emotions, feelings, and ideas. We must work to perfect the communication skills that bring legitimacy to our words and willingness on the part of our children to listen to us. Here are six helpful tips that have been proven to promote communication between parents and middle-years children or teens.

Tip One: Accentuate the Positive

In chapter 4, we talked about the fact that parents tend to spend more time and energy suppressing wayward behavior in their children than they do in elevating good behavior. We spend more time restraining wrong than advancing right. While words of restraint are necessary throughout the training process, we must retrain ourselves to communicate the positive. This will take self-discipline, but the efforts will pay great dividends.

When communicating with your children attempt to speak as often as possible in the positive, not the negative. If there is something you don't want your child to do, then communicate your desire for restraint by speaking in favor of what you want done. Here is a sample list to help you get in the habit of positive speech.

Instead of:	Consider:
Don't spill your cereal.	See how carefully you can carry your cereal bowl.
Don't get out of bed.	Obey Mommy and stay in bed.
Don't hit your sister.	You need to show kindness to your sister.
Don't talk so much.	You need to learn to become a good listener.
Don't chew with your mouth open.	Chew quietly with your mouth closed.
Don't leave a mess for someone else to clean up.	Be responsible and clean up after yourself.

With young children there will be plenty of justifiable "don'ts." "Don't touch the knives." "Don't play with the stereo." "Don't hit the dog." Such prohibitions are appropriate with young children. But the middle-years child is in need of positive direction. He will not get it unless you change the way you communicate your prohibitions. The prohibitions you are looking to establish *can* be communicated positively. Consider the transfer from negative to positive speech another middle-years transition—for you.

Tip Two: Create Opportunities to Talk and Listen

Children need to have access to Mom and Dad. It is important for our kids to know that we are open to what they have to say and that we will understand. If our middle-years children don't have the option of coming to us, they begin to take things into their own hands. They will come up with their own solutions for problems, often making choices that are not in their best interests.

At this point in your child's life, this may not seem like a critical issue. You may think your child knows he or she can come and talk to you. You take the fact that your preteen rarely does so as a sign that at this time, he or she has no real need for meaningful conversations.

Do not make the mistake of assuming there is no need. Your child must have deep, meaningful conversations with you. He or she may not be aware of the need, but it is there. Even when children realize they need to talk to Mom and Dad, they may not know how to make that happen.

You must create the opportunity for healthy talk and healthy listening. This may take some planning on your part. If you are extremely busy, you may need to schedule some time to sit down and talk. This may be especially difficult if you are not a talker. Perhaps you and your spouse can go for hours or days with minimal conversation. Your relationship is fine, you just aren't big talkers. Yet you may have a child who is a talker. He or she will need even more conversation than a child who is not.

Even quiet, reserved children, however, must learn to communicate and have conversation. It is likely that one day in the future, your child will choose to be married. Your success at engaging in family conversation today will dramatically impact his or her relationship with your future son- or daughter-in-law. You and your middle-years child must have times when you can talk.

This will become increasingly important as your son or daughter approaches the teen years. If he or she is now eight or nine years old, there will be less of a need than there will be between the ages of ten and twelve. However, you are still preparing for adolescence. Do not wait until the teen years are upon you to begin developing your communication skills. What you do today will help prepare the way for adolescence. There is no better time than now to begin. Start today to begin creating these four different opportunities:

Father Talk Times

It is vitally important that dads create time in which they can talk to their sons and daughters privately. This can be done through everyday activities. Go shopping together, throw a football, take walks, or go out to breakfast. No matter what the activity, these "together times" will provide incredible opportunities for conversation and bonding.

Mother Talk Times

Mothers often feel as though they do a lot of talking with their kids, particularly during the early years. However, communication is going to look dramatically different during the middle years. Moms must now allow their kids to do more of the talking, while they develop the skill of listening.

If you have been a talkative mom, you'll find that God is stretching you during these years as you must listen more. In the past, if you have been fairly quiet, you may have to learn to talk more. Or perhaps you're simply not very comfortable with the idea of having more equal conversations with your child. No matter what challenge you face, God is with you. Ask Him to help you learn how to have successful conversations with your child.

Father/Mother Talk Times

A child needs talk times that involve Mom, Dad, and him or her. As you move toward the teen years, this needs to happen on a regular basis. In our house, whenever one child stayed over at a friend's house for the weekend, we attempted to carve out some special time for the sibling left at home. As a trio, we would do something out of the ordinary. This situation provided a perfect opportunity to talk, listen, and find out what was going on in the life of this particular child.

Don't wait until problems arise before saying, "The three of us are going to talk." That will put your child on the defensive. If these talk times are happening on a regular basis, however, you will be able to use them as a conversation tool when serious talks do need to occur. Your child will feel comfortable in talking with Mom and Dad when it matters most.

Family Talk Times

In chapter 6 we talked about groupthink. Now we're talking about "familythink." Your middle-years child needs to know what your family thinks.

Meal times may now provide this opportunity for you. But in just a few years, this will most often occur at bedtime. Once your child gets his or her driver's license, it will be harder to find times when all family members are at home at the same time.

Whatever the time frame, plan now how you will create opportunities to communicate with your children. Don't wait until the middle of the teen years when you are scrambling for time to try to establish this healthy habit.

Tip Three: Be Sensitive to the Sorting Process

We're all familiar with the saying, "A picture is worth a thousand words." Today, we'd like to suggest to you that the "picture" your child paints for you while communicating is worth a million words. Why? Because it is through early conversations with Mom and Dad that he or she will begin to sort out life and relationships.

As we have already discovered, your middle-years child is

going through a number of transitions—moral, biological, and relational. Often new challenges in life are not easily harmonized with old, well-worn beliefs that have guided the child thus far. But now life is about to become even more complex. Sorting out the various issues of life is one of the primary tasks to be tackled in pre- and early adolescence. Often middle-years children talk at a surface level, but confusion lies at another. This is where gentle conversational probing comes in.

Sissy's Story

Although she didn't see her same-age cousins that often, eleven-year-old Sissy was always glad when their visit was over and they went back to their own house. Her mother picked up on the attitude and began to probe.

Mom: Honey, every time you find out your cousins are coming to visit you're excited. But once they get here, you seem agitated.

Sissy: Sarah and Kim are so bossy when they come over. We always have to do what they want.

Mom: Well, you know, honey, they are our guests. We want to be hospitable, and they only come for the weekend.

Sissy: But it bothers me.

Mom: Yes, it might bother you. But sometimes God brings people into our lives to teach us things. He wants us to learn patience and how to be kind to people who trouble us. All of this is to help us become more like Jesus.

At this point, Sissy's surface message was about her bossy cousins. Mom attempted to work this issue through with her child but sensed that something more was going on in Sissy's heart. She also realized that Sissy herself might not understand her own feelings. The dialogue continues.

Mom: Sissy, do you remember when you were a little girl? I used to hold you on my lap and we would talk about life. Would you let me hold you now? (Sissy moves to Mom's lap.) Honey, is there something more that's bothering you?

Sissy: I don't know.

Mom: But you understand how God can use people, even irritating people to help shape you into the person He wants you to become?

Sissy: I know that, Mom, but they always want to hang around with Brian and Daddy. I'm just in the way.

Mom: No, you're not in the way. But you have to remember, Sarah and Kim do not have an older brother or a dad living in the house. One of the reasons they like to come here is because they get to share Daddy and Brian with us.

Sissy: That's what I don't like about them coming. They're trying to get Brian and Daddy to love them instead of me.

Mom: Oh, honey. No one can replace you. You are very special to your brother and your dad. You will always receive their special love. No one wants to take that away from you. And even if they wanted to, it wouldn't be possible.

In this abbreviated, but true life story, it was Mom's sensitivity that was able to bring out Sissy's lingering attitude. It is sometimes difficult for a middle-years child, who is trying to sort life out, to see beyond his or her own fears. In Sissy's case her fear of displacement kept her from understanding her cousins' tremendous need for loving male guidance. Mom helped put all this into perspective for her.

Forcing their way into your preteen's rapidly expanding world are new relationships, emotions, attitudes, experiences, and sensations. They come in twisted and tangled and are in need of sorting out. Do you remember the uniformed gate agents of chapter 2 who greet arriving passengers and help them on their journey? During the middle-years phase of growth and development, your child will need your help in sorting out life. He or she will emerge from childhood into a world that sometimes does not make sense.

In the case of Sissy, there were two messages being communicated. When taken at face value, Sissy's initial words seemed to indicate that she was troubled because her cousins were bossy and wanted to spend more time with Brian. But when Mom began to dig below the surface, she found that there was much more to the situation than met the eye.

Listen for unspoken messages like these. Pay attention to *all* the signals your child is sending, through body language, facial expression, tone of voice, and an overall sense of urgency. These nonverbal cues will give you invaluable insights to the message your child is trying to communicate and the issues of life he or she is facing.

Tip Four: Have a "Ten-Talk"

Those of you familiar with our teen series have already been introduced to the concept of ten-talks. However, this information bears repeating because ten-talks are one of the most useful tools we've found to help aid in parent/preteen communication.

As parents, we are often busy when our kids need us. It's impossible to break away from the task at hand every time we hear the plaintive cry of "Mom?" or "Dad?" At the same time, we want to place the highest priority on our children and our relationships with them. Ten-talks help us to strike a healthy balance between the tasks at hand and our children's need for parental attention.

This is the way a ten-talk worked in the Ezzo household: When our children absolutely needed either Mom's or Dad's immediate attention all they needed to say was, "I need to talk to you, and this is a ten-talk." These words told us that there was nothing more important in Amy or Jenny's life at that moment than talking to one of us. At those times, we knew we needed to put down the task at hand and give our child the attention she required.

We also had other levels of talks, from nine-talks down to one-talks. An eight-talk meant, "I need to talk to you soon. Can you give me some time in the next half hour?" A six-talk called for time together that same day or evening. A four-talk required a response in the next few days. And a two-talk meant, "Dad, I have some questions. Could you get back to me whenever you get a chance?"

By teaching how to invoke a ten-talk, you are giving your preteen the responsibility of telling you what he or she needs. You are also communicating to your child, "I trust you. I know that you will give me an accurate picture of what you need."

This will not always be the case. Especially in the beginning, everything may feel like a "ten" to your child. Do not assume that he or she is not ready to learn about ten-talks. This is simply part of the training. Patiently tell your child, "Honey, that's not a ten. It's a seven. Let me tell you why." Explain that this is an issue another family member can help with or one that can wait until later. Then assure your child that you will give him or her your full attention in the appropriate amount of time.

If you have an introverted, phlegmatic child, you may experience the opposite problem. After being called to a three-talk, you may realize that the need was much more urgent than your child led you to believe. Again, simply explain the difference and assure your child that he or she can invoke an eight-, nine-, or ten-talk if there is a genuine need.

You may begin to teach ten-talks when your child reaches the age of eight or nine. The tool will be most useful as your child approaches the teen years and moves toward a place of moral maturity. However, as with most of the principles we are sharing with you, it is important to begin learning these skills now, during the middle years.

Tip Five: Guard Your Tongue and Tone

One day, twelve-year-old Barry came home from school with great news: the teacher had selected him to be first-chair trombone in his seventh grade band class. That evening when his dad came home from work, Barry ran into the kitchen and shouted, "Guess what, Dad! I made first chair!" Overcome with enthusiasm, he let his imagination soar and cried out, "I'm going to be a musician when I grow up!"

The feelings this announcement evoked in his father ranged from shock to sincere concern regarding his child's future. "Not if you want to make any money, you're not," he said sharply.

Barry's face fell. He hung his head and turned away. As his father watched him retreat from the living room, he realized he had made a grave error. His son had tried to share with him something that was of great importance to him. In his rush to protect his child, Dad had stolen the joy from his son's heart. In that moment, Barry did not need an analytical assessment about his career aspirations. He needed to share his accomplishment. He wanted Dad to enter into his sense of excitement.

Remember these two rules of thumb when responding to

your preteen: Measure your response against the expression on his or her face, and most of all, think before you speak.

We wish someone had shared this principle with us when we were young parents. I (Gary) remember the morning Jennifer came running into the house with an enormous pine cone. In her desire to share this discovery she set the item in question on the kitchen table and exclaimed: "Dad, look at it!" Her entire face was glowing with excitement, and she wanted to share that feeling with me.

In that moment I failed her and myself. What Jennifer saw was a beautiful treasure. What I saw was a mess. Disturbed, I turned to her and said, "Jennifer, get that thing off the table. It's full of ants and sand and goo."

In that moment I saw those words destroy a special moment in the life of my little girl. As I watched the joy and excitement drain from her face, I asked myself, Why? Why that tone? Why those words? Since that time I have learned this vital lesson that I now share with you. When your child comes to you with excitement and joy written on his or her face, make sure you guard your tongue and tone. If we fail our kids in their moments of discovery, we potentially lose more than the moment: We lose our children's sense of security and trust in knowing they can share life with Dad and Mom.

Tip Six: Show Your Child You Know the Feeling

At nine years old, Laura had already shown signs of true artistic ability. Drawing was one of her favorite activities and it made her feel good when others acknowledged her talent.

When she entered a school-wide poster contest, Laura became extremely excited. She worked hard on her entry for weeks and hoped she would win first prize. Instead, she placed third. Her disappointment was only increased by the fact that the selection committee gave top honors to her best friend, Molly. Not only did Laura feel a sense of loss, she struggled with feelings of resentment and jealousy.

Laura's mother, Sandra, knew exactly how Laura felt. She remembered a time in junior high when she had lost the leading role in her school play to her friend Dana. By sharing that story, and her own emotions, with her daughter, Sandra was able to help Laura through a difficult experience. She helped her daughter come to terms with her feelings, and even to find a sense of accomplishment in the fact that her work had been honored. Best of all, Laura was assured that Mom knew what she was going through. She had been there herself and she understood.

We do want our children to know that we understand. In moments such as the one described in the scene above, sharing with our kids a particular life incident is both timely and helpful. But there is another way to help prepare your children for the emotional roller coaster ride of adolescence. It comes by routinely sharing with your child stories about your life. Don't wait for a moment of crisis to occur. Make the stories you share a constant part of your relationship with your child. That way, when trials occur, your son or daughter can think, without your prodding, "This has happened to Mom, too," or "Daddy understands what I'm going through."

During the middle years, your child is undergoing a great transition. He or she is experiencing different, greater, and more complex emotions. Understandably, many kids lack confidence and develop feelings of inadequacy when they find themselves faced with new situations. Sometimes they feel emotionally isolated because they think (just as you did when you were their age) that Mom and Dad could never understand what they are facing.

Yet we all know that is not true. Although we grew up in a

different time and place, the emotions we experienced in our youth were just as real as the ones our kids feel today. Do your kids know that?

No one reaches adulthood without having experienced betrayal, an unkind word, rejection, disappointment, grief, joy, unexpected pleasure, and triumph. Attached to every one of these emotions is a personal story. Your child needs to hear your stories. He or she needs to know that you really do understand, and that you experienced these emotions long before they did.

There is something about sharing life stories with our kids that takes us beyond a mere desire to entertain and to be entertained. These stories communicate to our kids the assurance that they are not emotionally isolated in this world. They are reminded that others feel as they feel, and that they know the good and bad times as well as feelings of pain or joy.

Most powerful are the stories about Mom and Dad and their childhood. As adults and parents, we have already lived every emotion our children will experience. We all can share anecdotes from our past that reflect every one of these feelings. One story in particular helped our girls understand that their dad, Gary, fully understood the feeling of disappointment.

While baseball was the national pastime in the 1950s, as it is today, fishing was Gary's sport when he was a child. He loved to hit a stream or a lake for the day, and enjoyed himself more when he knew he could fish somewhere guaranteed to give him a day's catch. That's why he was excited to receive an invitation from the neighbors, Mr. and Mrs. Wadsworth, to join them the following weekend when they opened their cottage on White Birch Lake. It was bluegill heaven—a lake teeming with fish ready to hit anything offered as bait.

The Wadsworths had high expectations of going and told

Gary's parents they would call early on Saturday morning to confirm the invitation. If Gary's family did not get a call, however, that would mean the Wadsworths would be going some other time.

All week Gary looked forward to what the weekend would offer. On Friday night, he readied his equipment, dug his worms, checked his poles, and put out his boots. He was ready for what he had hoped to be a great day of fishing. At eight o'clock the next morning, the phone rang. Gary knew it was Mr. Wadsworth. The voice on the other end told his mom, "Get the boy ready. We'll be by in ten minutes."

"Ok," Gary's mom said, "he'll be ready."

He was going!

In less than two minutes Gary gathered his poles, worms, and tackle box, and dashed to the end of the driveway. There he stood, looking up the road, watching for the Wadsworths' silver 1950 Plymouth. It was springtime, the sun was shining, school was out, and life was good.

He waited five, ten, then fifteen minutes. He reminded himself about being patient. Older people in their forties are sometimes slow and forgetful, he told himself. They probably just forgot a few things. They'll be coming—he was sure of it!

After another twenty minutes, he began to wonder if something had happened. The Wadsworths only lived down the street.

Gary went into the house to ask his mom to call. Maybe there was some confusion. Maybe he was to meet them at their house. What if they were waiting for him? Even worse, Gary thought—what if they had left without him? His mom dialed the phone while he went back to the roadside.

Gary later found out how the conversation went.

"Henry, this is Anna Ezzo," his mom said to Mr. Wadsworth. "Gary's been waiting for you out front, ever since you called. Will you be coming by shortly?"

"Anna, there must be a mistake," Henry told her. "We never called you this morning. Something came up at the last minute, and we're not going up to the lake."

It was then Gary's mother realized the amazing coincidence. The first call was a wrong number. Whoever called just happened to say enough right things to make her think it was Mr. Wadsworth.

Today, Gary can still see in his mind's eye his mother walking down the driveway. He knew by looking at her face that he wasn't going. She told him about the first call and explained that he wouldn't be heading up to the lake after all.

All the hopes that a little boy's imagination could muster were dashed. He had already borrowed from anticipated excitement, only to be let down. In that moment, he knew disappointment, and he was overwhelmed by it.

Disappointment. It's the emotion felt when a person experiences something less than what they anticipated, were promised, or had planned on. Yes, on that May morning in 1957, Gary knew disappointment. Years later, he realized that his children would also face disappointments in the years ahead. He wanted them to know he understood, and he was able to use this story to help communicate that truth.

Your child needs to know that you understand what each emotion feels like. We do not advocate that you share all the horror stories from your life. You don't need to reveal the details of your past sins. However, your child needs to know that you understand feelings like sadness, jealousy, and betrayal. Here is a suggestion that can help you begin:

On a sheet of paper list what you consider to be the most common human emotions. Write down disappointment, joy, anger, hurt, rejection, and any others you may think of. Then think back to your own child-hood. Every one of these emotions can be illustrated by a story from your past. Write down one emotion and do a word study on it from the Bible. How did Old and New Testament characters deal with these feelings? Begin by sharing one of your personal stories with your child in the next week.

In doing so, you will instill in your child a confidence that Mom and Dad can relate—and that he or she can relate to you. This confidence will keep your middle-years child turning to you in the times of emotional turmoil that lay ahead.

SUMMARY

We all need to be able to communicate effectively. You may think you have a clear picture of your child's communication style, but during the middle years patterns of communication may change, and Mom and Dad need to be aware of this.

Thankfully, our God is a God of communication. The Bible reveals to us that He does have an opinion when it comes to the ethics of communication. Whether we are speaking or listening, we must keep our thoughts and actions related to communication in line with the truths in God's Word.

One of the best ways we can encourage our preteens is through healthy, proactive communication. Six rules to help us make this happen are: 1) Verbally communicate dos, instead of don'ts, 2) create opportunities to talk and listen, 3) be sensitive to the sorting process, 4) use "ten-talks," 5) guard your tongue and tone, and 6) let your child know you understand the feelings they are going through. All these approaches help us to communicate more sensitively and effectively with our children.

BRINGING IT HOME

1. Of the ethics in Scripture, which ones do you feel parents most commonly violate? Which ones do you most often violate?

2. What does it mean to listen for content and intent?

3. What must a child do before calling for a ten-talk?

4. What principle lies behind the suggestion to guard your tongue and your tone?

5. Why should you tell your children your life stories?

Chapter Ten

A WORD ABOUT
DISCIPLINE

Whenever we talk to parents of preschoolers, sooner or later all discussions seem to lead to one question: "How should I discipline my child?" Young parents want to know the best methods for controlling their children, how to establish and reinforce rules, and how to punish. We find it interesting that almost without fail, parents of preteens come back to that same question: "How should I discipline my child?"

Countless times, we have listened to the stories of moms and dads struggling to discipline their older children. There seems to be a prevailing assumption that if parents can master better methods of disciplinary correction, whether it be for a preschooler or a preadolescent, they will solve their parent/child conflicts.

This is simply not the case. Surely punishment plays a role in child training, but in the preteen and teen years it plays a greatly diminished role. As you read this chapter, remember that methods of correction and the means of encouragement cannot be isolated from the quality of relationship between parent and child. Each is dependent on the other. We know plenty of families that have great relationships between parent and child, but lack knowledge of proper discipline. Equally, we know other parents who know all there is to know about discipline, but lack a relationship with their kids. Right knowledge and right relationship are dependent upon one other.

Most age-related books such as ours eventually get around to the topic of discipline. *The Smart Parent* is no different. In this chapter, we will review the basics of biblical discipline, then move on to examine some methods of correction that will be particularly helpful during your child's middle years.

This chapter will not offer a sweeping and comprehensive review of the subject; the topic of child discipline is too complex to be contained in a single chapter. These are simply some solid teachings that will help you develop a greater understanding of the subject and assess your current approach to discipline.

At this time, we want to remind you of this vital truth: The more morally mature your child becomes in the months and years ahead, the less you will lead by your authority (including the application of correction) and the more you will lead by your relational influence. Now, before we get into some specific, age-related tips, let's review some foundational truths about biblical discipline.

BACK TO BASICS

Imagine for a moment that, after picking up your preteen at school, you decide to stop at a local fast-food restaurant to share a special treat with your child. You step up to the counter and order two hot fudge sundaes with nuts. Moments later, you sit down at the table together. Your child smiles innocently at you, then proceeds to bury his or her nose in the chocolate topping.

"Stop that!" you cry out in shock. But your words have no effect. Next, your child's fingers dig into the ice cream and act as miniature shovels. Within moments, the entire table is a sticky mess. "Don't!" you protest again, more quietly this time. You want your child to end this embarrassing behavior, but you are unwilling to put any "muscle" behind your command. You decide to watch and hold your tongue. Maybe there's no need to step in. Perhaps if you wait long enough, your child will discipline him- or herself.

Most, if not all, parents would agree that the adult described above is taking a ridiculous and ineffective approach to childrearing. A child who is not disciplined by Mom or Dad is not about to do so him- or herself. No child is endowed from birth with self-control, nor has he experienced enough in life to know how to govern his or her own behavior (Proverbs 29:15b). Parents fulfill the role of teachers, while children are disciples who learn from Mom and Dad a way of life (Proverbs 1:8–9).

As parenting educators, we are aware that the more consistent the discipline applied, the better adjusted and happier the child will be. We also know a basic understanding of the following principles will help any parent become more consistent and more confident in applying biblical discipline.

WHAT IS BIBLICAL DISCIPLINE?

While growing up in a Christian home, I (Gary) often heard the catchy phrase, Spare the rod and spoil the child. The proverb was seemingly quoted with divine authority by all adults. Only years later, after becoming a parent myself, did I discover the passage where the phrase originated. I was surprised to learn that it was not Solomon who penned those words but Benjamin Franklin, when writing *Poor Richard's Almanac.*

This misunderstanding illustrates a serious question about biblical discipline: How many Christians base their disciplinary habits on secular perceptions of biblical truth? The answer, unfortunately, is too many. The Bible exhorts parents to "discipline" their children. But our cultural understanding and practices rarely line up with a scriptural interpretation of the command. A child who disobeys may hear his mother say, "I'm afraid I'm going to have to discipline you for that." This is a common, but misused, application of the word. Today, we culturally define discipline to mean "spanking" or "punishment," but true biblical discipline refers to one thing: training of the heart. To limit biblical discipline to spanking and punishment distorts the intent of Scripture.

Parents, please understand this important truth: The core of biblical discipline is not punishment, but instruction. When Solomon was penning the Book of Proverbs, he referred to instruction approximately one hundred times, directly and indirectly. From the beginning of Proverbs to its end, instruction is the starting point of moral exhortation.

As a parent, what type of instruction do you give? Are you the type who only gives commands? Or worse, do you tend to be the permissive type who never gives any? Do your instructions teach the intellect but not the heart? Do you demand a new task of your children without showing them how to do it? Most methods of instruction have value, and they fulfill a learning purpose. There is a time and a place for each method, but the primary one should be moral instruction, which is best accomplished during periods of non-conflict.

In Deuteronomy 6:6–9, Moses addresses the heart of a parent: "And these words which I command you today shall be in your heart." The phrase "be in your heart" literally means to be as a weight on your heart, referring to a sense of urgency. In verses 7 through 9, Moses instructs parents to teach their children diligently and to do it during the course of daily activities.

Biblical discipline consists of a number of essential principles and actions: some encouraging, some corrective. Various forms of encouragement that complement the biblical process include verbal praise and rewards. The corrective side consists of admonishment and related consequences. Each activity has purpose, meaning, and a legitimate place in the overall process.

MISTAKES AND MALICIOUS INTENT

Children make mistakes and children do misdeeds. While the two statements sound similar, the differences between them are profound. The first speaks of nonrebellious acts that are in need of correction; the second speaks of a malicious intent to do wrong. There is a distinction between the child who accidentally hurts his brother while in the process of playing and the child who does so with the intention of inflicting pain. While the actions are technically the same, the presence or absence of wrongful motive determines the course of correction that should be taken.

Another way to consider the difference is to look at the words *childishness* and *foolishness*. We use *childishness* to refer to innocent immaturity. This includes those nonmalicious, nonrebellious, accidental mistakes our children make, such as spilling a glass of water, tripping over a lamp cord, or accidentally bumping into someone. *Foolishness,* on the other hand, implies the presence of evil motives, intent to defy authority, or a decision to hurt someone. In this case, motive plus action adds up to wrongdoing.

Parents should correct both childish mistakes and foolish defiance, but the form of correction, as well as motive and need for it, will differ between the two. Parents should begin by asking the following important question: "Was what my child did the result of an accident, or did it come out of a decision to defy authority or hurt someone?" How that question is answered will determine what happens next. Is there a need to correct only your child's action (childishness), or must you correct both action and motive (foolishness)?

CORRECTING CHILDISH MISTAKES

The primary reason we take time to correct our children's nonrebellious mistakes is to help them become responsible human beings. Whether a child accidentally steps on and crushes a flower, spills his glass of milk at dinner, or unintentionally breaks a window with his football, the need to teach personal responsibility is a societal obligation for Mom and Dad.

Depending on the mistake, correction may come in the form of a simple verbal warning. Olivia is generally characterized by hanging up her clothes or putting them in the hamper at the end of the day. Today, her mom found several shirts piled on the closet floor. For that rare offense, her mom admonished Olivia to put her clothes where they belong. That warning served to encourage Olivia to be responsible.

Some childish mistakes bypass the warning stage and require the employment of either natural or logical consequences to teach responsible behavior. One time, our own daughter, Amy, was playing in the living room when she accidentally tripped on the lamp cord. A moment later we heard the crash of porcelain. Although Amy did not mean to break the lamp, she was responsible for her mistake. We implemented a related and logical consequence to teach her to accept responsibility for her actions and to help her learn to make things right. She had to clean up the mess, and in this case earn some extra money to help pay for the lamp's replacement. As parents, we were motivated not by a need to punish Amy, but by a desire to help her understand that we are all responsible for our actions—even when we don't mean to hurt someone or break something.

When dealing with childish mistakes, natural and logical consequences are usually employed, rather than punishment. The parent is not attempting to set a value on evil behavior, for there is no evil intent to honest mistakes. But when dealing with wrong behavior, correcting the motive of the heart is as important as correcting the action, and that is where an understanding of punishment comes in.

When it comes to training our children, the employment of consequences—natural or logical—differs from the application of punishment. While the first approach helps a child take ownership for his or her nonrebellious acts, as it did in Amy's case, punishment sets a value on an offense. Through punishments, Mom and Dad make value statements. We are establishing in our children's minds the degree and seriousness of a wrongful act.

For this reason, both underpunishing and overpunishing are dangerous. If a child is punished with five minutes in the time-out chair after hitting and bruising his sister with a plastic bat, Mom and Dad have just established in the mind of the child that hurting other people is not a serious infraction. Unjust punishment can go to the other extreme. When a parent says, "You left your lights on after leaving your room, and for that you're grounded for a month," he or she is overpunishing the child. This fosters exasperation in the child and, ultimately, more conflict.

CORRECTING FOOLISH BEHAVIOR

Foolish behavior needs correction, but parents should not correct all foolishness the same way, or with the same strength of consequences. Parents should consider the following four factors when rendering a judicial decision about a child's foolish actions: 1)the frequency of the offense, 2) the age of the child, 3) the context of the moment, and 4) the overall characterization of behavior.

Since a child's foolish offenses range from infrequent and minor infractions to open defiance, correction should reflect the degree of the offense. Generally speaking, a child's foolishness falls into one of three levels: 1) minor infractions that call for a verbal warning and reminder, 2) infractions that need some action and which call for more than a verbal reprimand, and 3) offenses that require full correction through the use of age-appropriate punishment and natural and logical consequences.

Many forms of correction are applicable during middle-years training. Logical and natural consequences, loss of privileges, isolation, and chastisement (or spanking) are all appropriate forms of discipline. But by the time a child reaches the middle years, spanking should rarely be needed.

This concludes our discussion of discipline basics. Again, this not an all-encompassing discussion of the subject, but a review of some important truths. If you come away with one key thought, let it be this: There is really only one reason we discipline our children—their lives require training. Our kids need to learn to live safely, wisely, and in a manner that is glorifying to God. Their natural inclinations will not bring them to these conclusions. Parental guidance is necessary. That guidance is all part of discipline. In addition to the basic principles listed above, there are five specific middle years, age-appropriate discipline rules that are important for you to grasp.

Rule One: Correct Personal Attitudes through Substitution

Not long ago a young father said to Gary, "My son has a problem with jealousy. How do I punish him?" This specific question leads to a broader one. How do you correct the sinful attitudes of the heart? How do you help your child overcome the fleshly impulses of his or her humanity?

Because of their age, middle-years children are better served by substitution than suppression. The father mentioned above was frustrated by his failed efforts to suppress his son's jealousy. No matter how hard he tried to keep the lid on it, jealousy continued to leak out. Instead of suppressing the wrong, he needed to enhance the opposite virtue.

If you have a child struggling with envy, teach charity; for anger, teach self-control; for revenge, teach forgiveness. Using substitution, and not just suppression, will make all the difference in the world. The young father above finally did just that, and his son's jealousy was replaced by a newfound sense of contentment.

Rule Two: Teach Tomorrow's Consequences Today

Teach your children concretely by showing them tomorrow's consequences for today's decisions. The operative word above is *concretely.* There are some examples that must be absorbed by the senses if our children are to learn their lesson.

Katie and Matt, although fun to play with, were not trained to be responsible children. Our kids knew that from previous experiences. One Saturday afternoon while Katie and Matt were visiting Amy and Jenny, the four decided to play house. But instead of playing upstairs in the girls' rooms, Katie and Matt convinced Amy and Jenny to set up house outside in the woods.

We gave our children one warning: "Girls, everything you take out must be returned."

"Ok, Mom and Dad," came the response. We knew how this was going to turn out. Our kids should have known how it would turn out as well.

Amy, Jenny, Katie, and Matt began hauling small tables and chairs, play stoves, and play sinks to the woods alongside the house. Before long, an "Alice in Wonderland" tea party had begun. The kids had neatly placed little plates on the table, along with knives, forks, and napkins. The "kitchen" had pans on the make-believe stove, dishes alongside the pretend sink, and rocking chairs filled with stuffed animals—all under a natural canopy of oaks and maple trees.

The kids had been playing for about ten minutes when Matt and Katie's mom called them home. Amy and Jenny asked Katie and Matt to help them return everything to the house. Their request was greeted with an out-of-character desire by Matt and Katie to give their mother immediate obedience. "We gotta go. Our mother is calling." In that moment, the girls realized the mistake they had made as their guests left them sitting there with every item to put back themselves.

As Mom and Dad, we could have helped. We could have come alongside the girls, picked up some of their toys, and tried to teach into the moment. But we purposely chose not to. We wanted this lesson to sink in through their senses.

We directed the girls to return everything back to their rooms, just as they found them. When they were done, we sat and talked about unreliable friends. Our kids had already known that Katie and Matt were unreliable, yet they did not act on their discernment.

Every trip back to their rooms sealed a lesson that would serve them for life: One only needs to look at the fields of the fool to see where their counsel will lead (Proverbs 24:30–32). Teach your middle–years children by showing them concretely tomorrow's consequences for today's decisions.

Rule Three: Understand that Genders Have Different Needs

A number of years ago, Gary's mentor, Dr. Fred Barshaw, gave us some insights about communicating with sons. We needed his insights. He had sons and no daughters and we had daughters and no sons. This is what he taught us.

When parents attempt to correct a situation through communication, adolescent boys tend to feel more comfortable with *indirect* conversation. That is, instead of sitting down face to face, Dad or Mom should go outside with their child and work on the fence, tune up the car, or go to the workshop and finish painting the screens. When working on a common task with a parent, sons tend to listen without feeling threatened. They commit themselves to change more readily than when they are sitting on the couch talking through an issue.

Adolescent girls are just the opposite. They tend to feel more comfortable with direct conversation. That is, they seek heart-to-heart dialogue. In fact, if Mom said, "Here is the dish towel. You dry, I'll wash, and we'll talk about your troubling attitude toward your brother," the daughter would be less receptive than if the two sat together and talked face-to-face.

Remember these truths. Adolescent girls like direct, focused attention; adolescent boys tend to respond better to the indirect method. Getting the point across is the goal, not conforming your child to your preferred method of communication.

Rule Four: Understand Micro and Macro Rebellion

Rebellion can be defined as acts and attitudes of willful defiance. This includes disobedience, back talk, refusal to accept correction, and rejection of rightful authority.

Most kids demonstrate open rebellion. That is, when they cross the line, they cross it all the way. We call this macro rebellion—macro meaning large in contrast to small. For example, you tell your son to put the ball down gently, but instead he throws it at his sister. Or, you call your child to come to you and he ignores you, running off in the opposite direction. This is what we mean by macro rebellion.

There are a number of children who rebel in more subtle ways, being content to just put one toe over the line. These children fall into the micro rebellious category. That is, their sin is not clamorous, revealing, or as openly defiant as that of the macro child. The micro child is one who, instead of running away when called, will come over to you—half way. This is the child who, when asked to put the ball down, will put it in his or her pocket. When asked to stay out of the kitchen, a micro child will place both heels on the carpet and ten toes just across the floor tiles.

One distinguishing characteristic of this child is the fact that he or she rarely crosses the line in a macro sense. And that becomes part of the problem. Because the sin of the micro child just doesn't look too bad when contrasted with the sin of macro rebellious siblings, parents tend to underestimate the seriousness of the offense, dismissing it as just another minor infraction. But it is not a minor infraction to the child. For the micro child the toe over the line is one hundred percent rebellion.

A second problem follows on the heels of the first. The Bible says: "Because the sentence against an evil work is not executed speedily, therefore the heart of the sons of men is fully set in them to do evil" (Ecclesiastes 8:11). The results are found in verses 12 and 13: "Though a sinner does evil a hundred times, and his days are prolonged, yet I surely know that it will be well with those who fear God, who fear before Him. But it will not be well with the wicked; nor will he prolong his days, which are as a shadow, because he does not fear before God." The micro child has a false sense of God's judgment. Because the offense is dismissed as slight, the lack of correction breeds contempt for your authority—and for God's.

If you have a micro rebellious child who is still in the middle years, work diligently with his sin, lest his sin give him a false sense of comfort and confidence. Without correction, the dreaded consequences will show up during the teen years.

Rule Five: Do Not Parent to the Lowest Common Denominator

During a parenting seminar one mother told us: "Everything is going so well. I'm afraid if I let up on the oldest, the younger children will not understand why they don't have the same privileges." This mom needs to tell the younger children that when they become as responsible as their older brother or sister, they too will have those special privileges.

It is necessary that you grant freedoms to your child as he or she attains the age-appropriate level of self-control. It is true that when freedom is granted a child who is not guided by the amount of self-control necessary to handle those freedoms, ultimately that child becomes enslaved by his or her passions. In contrast, however, when freedoms granted a child are greater or less than the child's self-control capacities, a state of developmental imbalance is created. Please consider the following equation.

Freedoms granted that are less than a child's level of self-control = developmental frustration.

This truism refers to the fact that withholding freedom from a child who possesses age-appropriate self-control will eventually foster frustration. This is the warning we bring you regarding your middle-years child. In such cases, the child has the knowledge and ability to be responsible but not the freedom to apply these attributes. This combination indicates that Mom and Dad are being overly controlling.

We understand a parent's temptation to respond in this way. It is easy to lead by control, particularly if you have younger children in your home. If all of your kids are in the teen years, or all in the middle years, this does not cause as much tension. But if you still have toddlers, and maybe some just around five or six years of age, you still need to use parental authority with those children. If this is the case in your home, it will be tempting to treat your older ones the same way as you do the young ones. This is parenting to the lowest common denominator, and it is not in the best interests of your middle-years child.

This demonstrates yet another reason why we as parents must rely upon the Lord's strength: When we are working with a number of children at different age levels, we are constantly changing hats. Parenting to the proper age level is not easy, but it is vital to our children's growth. Remember Paul's admonishment in Ephesians 6:4 "And you, fathers, do not provoke your children..." Many parents frustrate their middle-years children by shackling them with the restraints they place on the younger siblings.

In a recent conference, another mother brought up this very point when she shared that she makes her nine year old go to bed the same time as his five-year-old brother.

"Why?" we asked.

The mother was very candid. "Because if I didn't, I would have a bedtime battle on my hands with the little one. And I don't want that."

Please Mom and Dad, don't do this to your middle-years child. Deal with the little brother, but not at the expense of withholding freedoms from your preteen.

SUMMARY

Many parents consider discipline to be a means of controlling a child's actions for the moment. That is true, but only partially so. The primary objective of discipline is long-term in nature. Any expedient actions that are taken must be in harmony with the overall objective. God's purpose for discipline is precise. Hebrews 12:11 states, "Now no chastening seems to be joyful for the present, but grievous; nevertheless, afterward it yields the peaceable fruit of righteousness to those who have been trained by it." Are you starting to see some of this fruit in your middle-years child? We pray that you will—soon.

Bringing It Home

1. Explain the difference between childishness and foolishness.

2. What is the first rule of correction?

3. How should a parent correct negative attitudes?

4. Do you have a micro or macro middle-years child? How is this demonstrated in his or her life?

5. Explain the following statement. Freedoms granted that are less than a child's level of self-control = developmental frustration.

Chapter Eleven

SEVEN WARNING FLAGS

For a family that so greatly enjoys ice fishing, living in Southern California has one obvious drawback—there's no ice. We remember our ice fishing days on Suncook Lake in New Hampshire. The sport could be the biggest bore when nothing was happening or the greatest thrill when the fish were striking. The signal that a fish had struck bait was the release of a red flag that would spring back and forth against the backdrop of white snow. The swaying flag called for immediate attention. Something was happening below the surface.

In middle-years parenting there are also certain red flags to look out for. These flags are signaling that something is happening below the visible water line of your child's life. None of these alone is necessarily a great threat. But as you see them begin to add up, you may feel considerable alarm and legitimate concern. These flags tell you that it is time for increased attention to your child's moral development.

In this chapter we have listed the seven most common warning signs and a short test to help you evaluate whether they have appeared in your family. Answer the seven questions about your child and add up the score based on the following scale. Then proceed to the explanation that follows. At the end of this chapter is a scoring evaluation that will allow you to measure the seriousness of the accumulated effect these behaviors and attitudes have on your child and family.

5 = This is very representative of our child
4 = This is usually representative of our child
3 = Sometimes this is representative of our child
2 = This is not usually representative of our child
1 = This rarely, if ever, is representative of our child

1. ____Our child does not follow the family standard when he or she is outside of our presence (or the presence of others who know and represent our family values).

2. ____Our child tends to enjoy friends more than his or her own family. He or she is always asking to bring a friend along on family activities.

3. ____The peers our child is attracted to come from homes that do not share our values.

4. ____We are starting to hear similar negative reports about our child from a number of different people.

5. ____Although it might be done in a playful way, our child continually seeks attention from the opposite sex.

6. ____Our child, upon receiving "no" from one parent, will go and ask the same question of the second parent without telling him or her that a "no" was already given by the first.

7. ____Our child shows a declining, not a growing, interest in spiritual things.

WARNING FLAG ONE

Our child does not follow the family standard when he or she is outside of our presence (or the presence of others who know and represent our family values).

We realize there is no such thing as absolute moral consistency among adults, let alone children. There is always a degree of discrepancy between one's personal moral code and one's behavior. But when your middle-years child becomes characterized by not caring who sees him doing something wrong, especially people who are familiar with your family's values, then the child's problem is one of shame, that is—the lack of it.

Shame, like empathy, is a moral emotion and one often confused with embarrassment. Shame and embarrassment, although similar, are not the same thing. During an interview, a woman notices a run in her nylons and immediately feels embarrassed. But there is no moral right or wrong to her situation.

In contrast, shame is triggered by moral circumstances. Before the fall of man, Adam and Eve were in the garden and they "were not ashamed" (Genesis 2:25). Shame is a mechanism of the conscience and acts as a restrainer of wrong behavior when personal moral conviction fails. That is, when the virtues of the soul are not sufficient to restrain temptation, God, out of protection for the society, provides the socializing tool of shame.

Many people are restrained from doing evil because they do not want social judgment to fall on them. Thus, shame becomes a societal safety net that is used when personal moral resolve is gone. Shame is motivated by the fear of judgment concerning one's conduct more than it is by the love of virtue.

Here is an example of what I mean: A friend of Gary's has his company name, "Bob's Lighting," abbreviated on his license plate. It reads, BOBLITES. He is fairly well known around town, so people often recognize his pickup truck. In a casual conversation one day, Gary asked him if it held him more accountable to the speed limit. His response was shamefully honest. "Yes, it does," he said. "I tend to drive faster than the law permits at times. But now that I have my vanity license plate, I think, What if people see me? I would be ashamed if they thought of me as a traffic violator."

In Bob's case, his desire to do wrong was negated not out of his love for virtue, but the fear of shame associated with being caught by the public. Bob is not alone. We all operate from a degree of potential shame. There are certain moral temptations that we turn away from because the impulse of public judgment is greater than the hatred for the sin that lies within our souls.

The moral makeup of our society complicates the problem even more. Today, our society is ruled by moral relativism. This means shame is no longer wanted or desired. If there are no absolute standards governing moral decency, in what context does shame respond? Without moral absolutes no behavior can be shameful.

That brings us back to your middle-years child. When a child does not follow the family standard outside of your presence or the presence of others who know and represent your family values, it is an indication that he has no shame. Certainly, when we were children, we did things outside the purview of our parents, but shame restrained us from doing wrong in front of adults who knew us and our parents. We were conscious of bringing shame to our parents and family. Today, the voice of shame, the safety net of our conscience is often lost. Make sure it's found in your child.

WARNING FLAG TWO

Our child tends to enjoy friends more than his or her own family. He or she is always asking to bring a friend along on family activities.

Children are social. They love companionship. At first, children merely want to do things with others. Those who satisfy this desire are playmates. As a child grows older, he seeks more than playmates—he seeks friends. As he matures into pre- and early adolescence, outside interests begin to expand and attachment to friends becomes deeper. But should outside friendships replace those inside the family? The answer of course, is no. But it does happen.

If a child's family offers him little satisfaction, he is deprived of the most important source of emotional security—his sense of belonging. When middle-years children fail to find relational satisfaction at home they turn outside the family to peers.

Parents need to be careful not to confuse a child's outward compliance to family rules as a mark of a healthy relationship. While it might be true that your child is a good kid who responds well and knows all the right things to do, such good behavior is not necessarily a true measurement of a good relationship.

One sign of this problem is a child's constant need for peer companionship, even during family times. This warning flag is pointing to your family structure. Are you cultivating an interdependent family, or have you drifted toward an independent family in which the individual's desires come before those of the group?

Children who are accustomed to receiving comfort and approval from a few intimate and dependable relationships such as found in the interdependent family, tend to look to those same or similar relationships for comfort and companionship as they move through adolescence. If this is not the case with your child, it is time to take inventory of your family structure.

WARNING FLAG THREE

The peers to which our child is attracted come from families that do not share our values.

Many years ago, we crossed the United States by car. We headed for Los Angeles and camped along the way. We pulled into our last camp site at 6:30 P.M., on July 18, 1983. Sitting up on a rise ten miles outside of the city of Las Vegas, our last KOA facility overlooked the brown heat waves rising from the city.

It was nearly nightfall when Gary finished pitching the tent. The business of the evening kept us occupied—so much so that we failed to notice the transformation of the city below. It was only after we sat down at our picnic table that we saw to the west the mysterious, luring lights of Las Vegas. We sat amazed. More than amazed, we were charmed, enchanted by the glittering scene below. Las Vegas was calling us to investigate her glamour.

Four thousand years ago another man pitched his tent on an elevated plain that overlooked a city. The man's name was Lot. The city was Sodom. Surely that city was not representative of the values Lot's uncle Abraham had instilled in him. Nonetheless, Lot found the city attractive, so much so that he left the plains and moved to the city to take up a new identity.

What drives a child to homes of differing values? Two things: First, the inherent attraction to that which is different, and second, the natural bent of some children to the more colorful aspects of life. The warning we now issue concerns itself with a possible misplaced identity, which leads to a misplaced allegiance.

Identity defines us by providing a set of socially understood reference points. The religious identity of a parish priest, for example, is revealed in his clothing, speech, and lifestyle. The rock musician also is recognized by his clothing, speech, and lifestyle. These two men have identities that complement their values, and both are identified by what they believe and how they act. People don't look at the rock musician and say, "Ah, there goes a religious man," nor do they look at the priest and say, "There goes a rock star."

Our identity associations reveal us for who we are and

what we believe. That is why parents need to monitor the types of peer attraction to which their child is drawn. This may be a red flag warning that your family identity is not all that it should be.

WARNING FLAG FOUR

We are starting to hear similar negative reports about our child from a number of different people.

"No, my son isn't really lying," said Brian's mother. "He just likes to tell stories." This parent refused to acknowledge her son's sin and so it was never dealt with.

It's true, some children are very creative. At times, creative stories can be confused with lies. But if a number of people are coming to you with this type of information—public or private school teachers, Sunday school teachers, people who watch your children on a regular basis—carefully consider their words.

Our school administrator was not the first one to approach this parent about Brian's dishonesty. Over time, many others had echoed a similar concern. Ever since his preschool days, Brian's appetite for the convenience of dishonesty had been dismissed by Mom and Dad. Only when the police started routinely knocking on the door did Brian's parents start to listen. By then it was too late. Their refusal to investigate, let alone accept any criticism of their son's behavior, helped shape him into a pathological liar.

It is humbling, embarrassing, and sometimes shameful to hear negative reports about our children. It's also difficult to accept some of these things when we have not seen such evidence for ourselves. Every bit of pride calls for us to dismiss the possibility that what we are hearing is true. To receive criticism about ourselves is never pleasant. To receive criticism about our children is even more painful. But if you are living and participating in a moral community, such a rebuke is an expression of God's grace. He cares for us. God sends people to us to warn and rebuke us. The Bible says, "Faithful are the wounds of a friend" (Proverbs 27:6).

Do not be like Israel. When the prophets came to speak to the Israelites' sin, they were dismissed and their words were ignored until the day of calamity. When friends start to bring similar reports to you about your child, listen to them.

WARNING FLAG FIVE

Although it might be done in a playful way, our child is continually seeking attention from the opposite sex.

This is a warning flag to Dad, in particular. It is a sign that there is simply not enough physical touch taking place within your family.

In the course of our travels, we visit many families. In some homes we find children who are starved for physical affection. It's not that the parents are purposely neglectful, but that other urgent demands dominate their lives. As a result, their children's need for touch goes unmet. Sometimes we are not in a home more than five minutes before children hop into our laps, seeking to be cuddled. Silently they are telling us, "Would you hold me? My dad is too busy." Many little boys and girls have all the material advantages of life, yet lack what they really need—routine embraces. If their need for physical affection is not met at home, children will seek to have it met elsewhere, often in sexual ways.

As your child approaches the teen years, he or she will demonstrate a growing interest in the opposite sex—this is natural. Some flirtation is normal and a certain amount should be expected. But is your child seeking sexual attention from others? If so, this red flag is an indication that there is a need for more attention, especially from Dad.

WARNING FLAG SIX

Our child, upon receiving "no" from one parent, will go and ask the same question of the second parent without telling him or her that a "no" was already given by the first.

Do you remember doing this when you were a kid? I think we all tried this. Many kids do this without feeling guilty. This flag is a warning that your child has not been sufficiently trained to the principle of the law. He or she is trained only to the letter of the law. This child is moral on the outside, but not necessarily on the inside.

In this child's eyes, getting a parent to approve the request satisfies the law. This stands above any guiding principle of how permission was gained. There is an outside legal morality at work, rather than an inside heart morality. To the child's way of thinking, the ends (gaining parental approval) override the means (the trickery that helped secure the approval). This is a warning flag. If your child is characterized by such behavior, your child has not yet internalized principles of godly behavior.

WARNING FLAG SEVEN

Our child shows a declining, not a growing, interest in spiritual things.

The child who shows a declining interest in spiritual things often does so because he knows all *about* God, but he does not personally know God. He may have lived off of the family's experience of God but not his own. As a preadolescent, your child will clearly begin to demonstrate independent movement toward God (apart from the direct influence of Mom and Dad) or a gradual drift away from Christian behavior.

Here are some healthy indicators of spiritual vitality you should look for. By the time your child reaches the end of the middle years, you can take comfort if you see some of these signs:

- quiet times
- prayer list
- personal ministry service
- desire for Christian fellowship
- comfort with discussions about the Bible
- growth in moral application

Challenge your child with these indicators and do not assume that because a profession of faith was made at five years of age that he or she is saved. Entertain the possibility that maybe this is not the case. Your child may have made a group decision in Sunday school, but not a true heart change.

If your middle-years child has not made a profession of faith between the ages of eight and twelve, the time has come to press for salvation. In saying this, we are not stating that you should force your beliefs on your child. However, salvation must become an urgent issue in your prayer life, one that you communicate to your child. Pray that your child will accept Jesus Christ as Savior. Not Mom and Dad's Savior, *his* or *her* Savior.

If a decision for Christ has already been made, watch for signs that your child is working out his or her salvation. You may be asked, "How can I know I'm saved?" Rather than sitting down and presenting the whole gospel presentation, have your child walk through the thought process with you. Ask: "What do you think? What does the Bible say?" then give your son or daughter an opportunity to answer. As he or she takes ownership, the concept of salvation will become more real.

It is fitting that we bring this chapter to a close with some final thoughts about salvation. The word *salvation* is the all-inclusive word of the gospel. It brings together the concepts of justification, redemption, grace, propitiation, imputation, forgiveness, sanctification, and glorification. The place where God claims lost people is at the cross. The cross is where Jesus died the death that we, by all rights should die, and would die, apart from Him. Many children raised in Christian communities have a clear knowledge of God but may not know Him personally. They need to be saved.

Jesus Christ said, "I am the way, the truth, and the life. No one comes to the Father except through Me" (John 14:6). The Bible tells us that, "He who has the Son has life; he who does not have the Son of God does not have life" (1 John 5:12). Furthermore, the Bible proclaims, "That if you confess with your mouth the Lord Jesus and believe in your heart that God has raised Him from the dead, you will be saved. For with the heart one believes to righteousness, and with the mouth confession is made to salvation" (Romans 10:9–10).

Parents cannot raise godly children apart from regeneration. The Bible warns of this. We know in the last days there will be those who "having a form of godliness but denying its power" (2 Timothy 3:5a). Jesus warned against the false assumption that you can become godly through training. He spoke against the righteousness found in those who trust themselves to be positionally righteous or justified because of their moral accomplishments (Matthew 23:28; Luke 16:15, 18:9). He taught that the truly justified (i.e., the godly) are those who acknowledge their sin and trust in God for forgiveness and His righteousness (John 14:6; Luke 18:9–14; Romans 3:23, 27–28).

Apart from a personal commitment to Christ, the fullness and purpose of life will always be in doubt. Both the motive and reality of righteousness are always in question. Becoming godly is a personal decision, not a parental one. Does your child know the Lord?

SUMMARY

As your child grows through the middle years, there are several warning flags which you can see that may indicate a need for increased attention to your child's moral development. One warning flag may not give you cause for alarm; however, several flags may be an indication that future problems will occur.

Watch for these signs: Your child does not follow the family standard when outside your presence; he or she enjoys friends more than family; your child is attracted to children from homes that do not share your values; you are beginning to hear similar negative reports about your child from a number of sources; your child continually seeks attention from the opposite sex; your preteen does not accept "no" for an answer and will try to get a different answer from your spouse, without telling him or her that you have already said "no"; your son or daughter shows a declining interest in spiritual things.

Jesus Christ wants your child's heart, not just his or her head. It is eternally important that you make sure it is not just head knowledge and intellectual assent your son or daughter has given to the Lord. Christ commands a complete surrender of heart and life in order for us to be truly born again. Your child needs to be saved, God's way.

BRINGING IT HOME

1. Take a minute to add up your score from the test at the beginning of the chapter.

My child's score is _____

2. Compare your score to the numbers listed on the scale below. In another year, take this test again, just to see where you are. Remember—one of these flags, by itself, is not a

major problem. But if you start seeing a number of these red flags, you possibly have trouble on the horizon as you move into the teen years. Take care of these "little" issues now.

Scores

7–9   You're doing great.

10–14   You're doing well, but stay watchful of the little behaviors.

15–20   Future conflict and crisis is on the horizon. There is still time to make course corrections and adjustments.

21–35   Future conflict and crisis imminent. Immediate changes needed.

3. Talk about this score with your spouse and, if appropriate, your children.

4. Discuss with your spouse, a friend, or a parent what you see as strengths and weaknesses discovered as a result of this test.

A FINAL WORD
OF ENCOURAGEMENT

O h, the joys of parenthood. Our children delight us with their laughter and humor, surprise us with their imaginations, and amaze us with their perception. Through their growing sense of wonder, they renew Mom and Dad's sense of adventure. Through their continual dependence on our care, they make us feel important. More than that, with their tender smiles and warm hugs, they make us feel loved.

Oh, the frustrations of parenthood. Our children have a knack of saying the wrong things at the wrong time in front of the wrong people. They throw our orderly world into disarray. When we plan an event weeks in advance, that is the exact day they get sick. They track in mud seemingly only after the floor is washed, and stain only their new clothes, nothing old. They humble us in public and make us feel like failures in private. This, too, is parenthood.

There is no avoiding this truth: Parenting is (to put it gently) a challenge. Children of all ages have needs and as they grow their needs become more complex. Naturally, as parents we want to meet as many of these needs as possible. But while striving to do so, we must be careful not to attempt to meet them in our own strength. Remember what we said in chapter 6: We cannot parent by our own strength and still achieve a godly outcome.

If this is true, however, upon whose strength *can* we rely? The authors of a best-selling book? Our children's teachers? The couple next door? As helpful as these resources may be, they are not sufficient in and of themselves. If we place our confidence in our own abilities or the abilities of others, we will be too stressed out, too tense, and too anxious to enjoy the parenting process or, more tragically, our children.

Moms and Dads, we urge you to settle this in your mind now: You will never have perfect children. None of us will. This is true in part because there is no such thing as a perfect parent, regardless of how many resources are made available to us. However, we do have a perfect God whose grace takes up the slack of our failures.

Be encouraged by the apostle Paul's words: "And He said to me, 'My grace is sufficient for you, for My strength is made perfect in weakness.' Therefore most gladly I will rather boast in my infirmities, that the power of Christ may rest upon me. Therefore I take pleasure in infirmities, in reproaches, in needs, in persecutions, in distresses, for Christ's sake. For when I am weak, then I am strong" (2 Corinthians 12:9–10).

This verse is true for all of us, even Moms and Dads. If we remain faithfully obedient to our parental duties, if we take seriously the calling to bring up our children in the nurture and admonishment of the Lord (Ephesians 6:4), we can be confident that God will use us in our weakness, to bring forth His fruit in His time. More than anything else we have shared with you in these pages, this final truth supersedes them all: With the grace of God on your side, you can enjoy your children now—and forever.

Maranatha.
Gary and Anne Marie